THE COURAGE OF A UKRAINIAN FAMILY

REFLECTIONS FROM AN ENGLISH HOST

ALICE WHITE

To Kathy

x Alice x

The Courage Of A Ukrainian Family -
Reflections From An English Host
By Alice White

ISBN: 978-1-7390972-3-3

Published by Gossage Vears Publications, 2023

Edited by Siân-Elin Flint-Freel

Formatting and Cover design by Irish Ink Publishing

Some names have been changed to protect identities

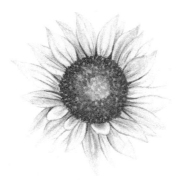

To Diana and Alya,
and all the brave Ukrainians who trusted us here in the UK with their
care.

"Do you know what words are without actions?
Lies. They are lies."
Deanna L. Lawlis

CHAPTER 1
THE KEYS

Two happy, relieved and tired faces are smiling back at me, and I think Luna is smiling too as only a contented cat can. As they triumphantly hold up their keys to their new apartment, I am so happy and proud for them and feel privileged to have played a small part in their journey to safety.

CHAPTER 2
THE IDEA

SOMETIME AROUND THE END OF MAY, 2022

I had been volunteering as a home visitor for a charitable refugee organisation for several years. The organisation connects people with a spare room in their home to refugees and asylum seekers coming to the UK in need of temporary accommodation.

I had one – a spare room that is – but so far, the need for accommodation had been mainly for families of three or more. In my small, two-up, two-down cottage, my second bedroom – mainly used when my granddaughter came to stay – would not really have been suitable for more than a couple of nights, and even then, it would be a squeeze for more than one person. Aside from that, most people were seeking shelter in the bigger cities where they may have relatives already settled.

So, I contented myself with making the home visits required to a few prospective hosts in and around my local area who could more adequately provide accommodation for their guests. This 'work' was second nature to me; having previously worked as a district nurse for many years, I was used to visiting people in their own homes. Discreetly checking out suitability, along with noting any potential hazards or needs that might arise before their guests arrived, was just an added element to my visit. However, I had never quite let go of the hope that I might one day be a host myself and welcome guests of my own.

Like so many others, I was touched deeply by the news reports on the war in Ukraine. The first I'd heard of it was in February 2022, when Russia invaded the country. I believe the conflict had actually begun many years before and if I'm honest, it was not something I had ever understood or taken much interest in.

Therefore, to me, it all seemed to develop so quickly and the news stories were (and still are at the time of writing) many and harrowing. Drawn to watching them and at the same time not wanting to see – a little like when you pass an accident on the motorway. I witnessed the horrors of parents clinging to their children, trying desperately to escape but also reluctant to leave their homes, parents, husbands, jobs, other family members and beloved pets. Their dilemma was inconceivable and almost tangible when it shockingly gatecrashed my living room via my television screen usually reserved for much lighter and indeed fictional stories.

This was disturbingly real.

I thought of my own small and cosy home with my long and wild garden. My two white cats (eight-year-old twins who I had rescued from a violent abusive home): Gabriel – the big, muscular and affectionate boy who nips me on my arm from the table where he sits as I squeeze past in my tiny kitchen between the table and the fridge, or he might dab me with his paw – a little too hard sometimes

– to remind me of his right to my attention; his sister Lily, much tinier and appearing fragile and shy, but she is in fact the braver of the two and the intrepid, patient and relentless hunter of mice and birds which she brings me in abundance – usually headless but sometimes alive and paralysed with fear. I end up spending more time than I can in reality spare, to nurture and revive them then searching to free them to a place of safety away from their hunter's teeth. My ten-month-old puppy, Rosso: friendly, licky and bouncy – a relatively new addition to my family and still establishing his place in the pecking order. He follows me everywhere – even into the toilet – and sleeps on my bed (just for his reassurance, of course). My ten chickens and a cockerel: not particularly friendly but extremely noisy at all hours of the day and night (I swear he crows in his sleep) and who have the luxury of the freedom to roam in my garden (Avian flu outbreak permitting).

This household, although lively at times, of course is peaceful compared to the traumas of a war-torn country. I felt grateful and yet at the same time slightly nauseous when I considered my insular and privileged life. And then the opportunity came…

This story is an honest account of what happened when three humans and several animals from very different cultures attempted to live together in harmony. What follows is a collection of diary entries, reflections and experiences drawn from what happened next.

CHAPTER 3
THE DECISION

FRIDAY, 3RD JUNE

My morning game of Wordle frustratingly isn't going well when a BBC News alert pops up on my screen. 'People are now invited to sign up under the government's Refugee Resettlement Scheme to host those arriving or attempting to arrive in the UK from Ukraine.'

I abandon hope of guessing the elusive five letter word (again surrendering the glory of victory to my friend Susan) and focus on what turns out to be an even more frustrating experience – trying to sign up on the government website, which has clearly already crashed under the pressure of people's burgeoning interest. I battle on for some time as I watch the search bar crawl like a depressed snail across my screen, only to find it replaced with the message, 'The page you are trying to reach is not available. Please try again later' flicker on and off like a light bulb about to expire. At one point, I actually manage to get my name and address into the form only to see it disappear again when I get to the next page. Grr! F*%ing useless government who promise something and then can't deliver! I give up and start my day's work as a psychotherapist.

My first client of the day is via a Zoom video call. While I wait for them to 'come into the room' I realise I haven't switched off my Twitter notifications. A couple of tweets pop onto my screen – people sharing their frustration at not being able to sign up to help – so I'm not alone and this gives me a useful reminder that I must indeed try again later.

I'm not the sort to give in easily. It's my coffee break. I search to see if there is a Facebook page for refugees trying to get to my local area and I'm pleased to see there is. Run by volunteers, this seems much better organised, but I'm still aware I need to go through the legal routes, although it looks like I might get some useful information and connections here to add to what I can glean from the government website (when/if I can ever get the damn thing to work). Being dyslexic does not help me to be enthused about what I imagine will involve negotiating endless bureaucratic policies and procedures, and I much prefer the 'person to person' contact of social media where I can 'see who I'm talking to.'

And see them I did. Post after post of bravely smiling faces clearly photographed in happier, sunnier times, many in the beautiful Ukrainian countryside before the horrors of war devastated their homeland. Some posts directly from the families seeking refuge, others shared by people who wanted to help. It makes for heartbreaking reading. Families marketing their personal attributes, reeling out their CV – sometimes in broken English, sometimes Ukrainian (where I had to use the social media platform translator to make sense of them), as they might when at a job interview. "We are clean people – churchgoers." "We don't drink." "We are just seeking safety." Often touting for the work that they hope to resume in the UK if they are lucky enough to get here: "I am a lawyer/a doctor/a beautician."

I feel shame that they are driven to promote themselves in this almost humiliating way in order to obtain their basic human right of safe refuge. Understandably, it seems there are still only families – no single people I could consider accommodating in my small space – and in any case, what's the point of getting their/my hopes up as I still haven't managed to sign up to register my interest?

REFLECTION:

Not sure how I am feeling about the religious references as a non-believer, and wondering how or if I will get along with people who don't like the occasional ~~bottle~~ glass of wine? Becoming aware there are cultural differences I hadn't anticipated. Typical me – heart before head.

CHAPTER 4
THE BREAKTHROUGH

SATURDAY, 4TH JUNE 3 A.M.

Another restless night – they are becoming all too familiar since I first heard of this terrible war – I have given up on sleep with my mind not able to be free of the horrors I have seen on the TV last night – so I give the government website one more try. I turn on my iPad – always by my bed, although usually reserved for more pleasant browsing and the occasional late-night film. (When I say film, to be more accurate, I mean the first half of films I have attempted to watch before falling asleep, only to try to pick them up again the following night.)

Having spent at least ten minutes frustrated with much overemphatic clicking on my tablet, I am pondering (half-awake, half-asleep) on how many other people might be sharing my inability to sleep. Suddenly – I can hardly believe it – something must have shifted in the atmosphere, and I jolt as the ping of the confirmation email lands.

'Thank you for registering your interest in hosting a refugee from Ukraine…'

Now all I have to do is make contact with one.

REFLECTION:

My mind is buzzing with excitement. What will my life look like in a few weeks'/months' time? Have I done the right thing? What will it be like to share my life and my home with someone after all these years of being alone?

CHAPTER 5
THE WAIT
(WHICH, IN REALITY, ISN'T MUCH OF A WAIT)

MONDAY, 6TH JUNE

Barely a day has passed, and now I have taken the first step towards my big decision, I am already getting impatient while waiting for the next stage. I experience that old familiar surge of dogged determination to make things happen and quickly, and yet the seriousness of the task – without anyone close to consult – is daunting.

I am not deterred even though my house and garden already often resemble a chaotic zoo. Surely another human living here won't make any difference. I've lived on my own for more than twelve years since the difficult break up of a four-year relationship and almost convince myself that I like it. Since then, not wanting to fit around others' needs, my erratic working hours and mealtimes do, in the main, suit me. I wonder what my previous long-term partner of twenty-five years, Dave, would have said, and wish for a moment that he was still alive and here to advise and support me in his ever calm and rock solid way.

Instead, I glance across at Rosso, who is curled up in

his usual spot on the sofa. Hopeful of some guidance, I say (albeit in a whisper), "Do you think I've lived on my own for too long?"

Getting nothing back aside from a soulful look from his big brown eyes peeping out from beneath his russet fringe, I settle on focusing on the more negative side of my independent lifestyle and consider how my life might be getting rather narrow. Taking a Ukrainian guest will surely broaden my cultural understanding with the possibility of gaining different perspectives and even new friends.

REFLECTION:

I have always felt a temporary buzz of satisfaction when donating money to charity. However, earlier this year, when I robotically clicked 'send' to donate to the Red Cross Ukrainian Crisis Appeal, it just didn't seem enough. I was aware I didn't quite get the buzz, feeling strangely empty. I guess if most of us were to speak honestly, donating makes us feel good – absolves our guilt, giving us permission to forget the traumas others are experiencing once we have contributed.

20 years! How could I have forgotten? Today would have been your birthday. Happy Birthday, Dave! Night night, sleep tight – love you.

It might be OK to have some company now – all this talking to myself can't be healthy, so in all honesty, I know my actions are not entirely altruistic.

CHAPTER 6
THE MATHS

TUESDAY, 7TH JUNE MORNING

My early morning mug of tea is as usual fuelling my trawl through the Facebook pages when I come across a post from a woman living quite near to me who is planning to sponsor a woman from Ukraine, due to arrive in the UK shortly. However, her forthcoming guest's boyfriend also wants to travel with her but the woman only has space in her home for one person. I do not feel comfortable taking a lone male so I message her to see if we could perhaps do a swap – I'd host the woman and she the woman's boyfriend. While I am waiting for a reply, I'm drawn to another post from a man (George) who is trying to support a Ukrainian woman, Diana, and her fourteen-year-old daughter, Alya, in completing their journey to the UK from The Netherlands. It sounds quite an urgent request as they only have another few weeks' permission to remain there.

I have no idea why, but my instinct tells me these could actually be 'my guests'. My excitement at this possibility quickly turns to panic – surely I don't have room for two!

However, undeterred by this minor detail, I jump up and distractedly throw my still half-full mug of tea into the sink. The clatter prompts Rosso to jump to his feet too and he looks around anxiously to see what the potential threat is that I may need him to protect me from.

The fact that a sofa I once bought on a whim required me to have it airlifted through a bedroom window as it wouldn't fit through the doors gives you some idea of my capacity to assess space. Undaunted, I rummage through that kitchen drawer – you know, the one we all have that contains all the odds and ends – and under the crumpled paper napkins, bits of candle and several keys that don't fit any locks of mine, I find my trusty tape measure. I rush up the narrow stairs, Rosso scampering behind me, always willing to help in whatever way he thinks he might be able to. (On this occasion, his help consists of trying to steal and chew the tape measure.)

In my spare bedroom, I take various measurements in a pointless attempt to try to estimate how much space two people will need to live comfortably in the room for several months. With a distant memory of a vague and probably totally irrelevant maths formula to calculate area – maths was never my favourite subject at school – I grab a pen and paper and scribble a few lines to get some perspective on how I might rearrange the furniture.

I send George a private message. He replies almost immediately with an invitation to join a WhatsApp group for the four of us to communicate and gather some more information about each other. I repeat the room calculation process on several more occasions during the day (as if the time of day makes a difference) in between my client sessions, mainly to while away the time until I can meet with George and my potential guests.

REFLECTION:

I think I'm trying to convince myself that hosting in this small bedroom, with a bit of readjustment, surely will be doable. All these calculations are pointless really as I know in my heart there is no going back for me now – I will find a way.

CHAPTER 7
THE LOGISTICS

TUESDAY, 7TH JUNE AFTERNOON

In the meantime, George's messages inform me that Diana and her daughter are currently living in one room in a hostel with shared kitchen and bathroom facilities – it's not clear with how many others. I imagine they have developed a very strong mother and daughter bond, both because of their close proximity on their travels and the traumas they have experienced, witnessed or have heard were happening back in their homeland since they left it. Understandably, they would want to stay close to each other after their distressing journey from firstly Ukraine to Slovakia and then to The Netherlands.

Having no idea at this point what I am doing or indeed how to do it, I refer back to the government website for advice and to see how to validate my potential guests' authenticity. I have met the (at least basic) legal criteria required for hosting when my application was accepted:

I am over 18 – ✅

I hold a British Passport – ✅
I do not have a criminal record – ✅

As usual, my optimism, enthusiasm and resolve to make this work overrides any concerns (real or imagined). However, I do need to take some responsibility to ensure to the best of my knowledge that they will not be breaking any laws either. The thought they could be sent back to Ukraine once they had got this far is unimaginable and I need to follow the guidelines carefully.

I search meticulously through the endless pages on the website as to how to proceed – really having to put in an extra effort to untangle the guidelines and regulations that are clearly not written with dyslexic brains such as mine in mind. From the documentation my potential guests willingly volunteer and George has forwarded, it appears they have the right to enter, remain and work in the UK for six months. Thinking ahead (unusual for me, I know), I understand from some of the Facebook posts exchanged between hosts clearly further ahead in the process than me, that should they wish to stay any longer they will need to be granted the mysterious (and I later realised elusive) BRP[1] by The Home Office.

I usually cannot remember the order of the letters in acronyms and I often change them into memorable words – in this case, 'Burp'.

REFLECTION:

I'm imagining it would be an offence to unknowingly assist illegal immigrants to come to the UK but I don't really know much more than that about it. Aside from a couple of parking offences, I don't want to spoil my unblemished record thus far. How do I know I can trust George?? Would I be responsible if the law was broken? I will run my thoughts by my therapist, not because I think she will know the law, but to look for reassurance I am doing the right thing. Close as I'm sure Diana and her daughter are, the small room I'm offering might be pushing the limits a bit.

Busy work day tomorrow. Still no message from Diana to say she has joined the chat group and loads to do in my now additional new 'job'. Maybe she's found another sponsor? I knew it was too good to be true.

1 Biometric Residence Permit

CHAPTER 8
THE FELINE SURPRISE

WEDNESDAY, 8TH JUNE

It is 12.35 p.m. (between client sessions), I have a sandwich in one hand and a pen in the other. I'm trying to catch up on some client note writing. Ding! A message from Diana! She's clearly joined the group chat.

I excitedly click on the profile photo that sits alongside her message to enlarge it, hoping this might be my first sighting of my potential guests. However, as the blurry image on my computer screen gradually clears, the stunning orange eyes that stare back at me are not of two humans as I am expecting, but of a cat – and a rather evil looking cat at that!

Then follows several more messages in quick succession.

Ding!

Ding!

Ding!

We are very grateful to you.

Ding!

God bless you.

Ding!

We are not happy here – I want to work and my daughter wants friends.

And then.
Ding!

We need to get to the UK right away.

Ding!

We cannot leave our cat – she is part of our family.

Before I can thank George for 'doing his bit' by introducing us, (or indeed ask him any further questions) I notice he has left the WhatsApp group.

REFLECTION:

I'm touched and concerned by the gravity of their desperation in equal measures. Did I miss that George had mentioned a cat?? This is going to take some doing and I am a pushover when it comes to cats. I'm beginning to doubt now with even more certainty that my spare room is going to be suitable, especially with this additional feline 'guest'. Their excitement is almost tangible from their responses. Do they also sense my doubts?

I am feeling a little alone now. George probably didn't want me to ask any awkward questions to explain why two guests had suddenly become three. Here I go making assumptions – he's probably very busy helping other people or maybe he thought I'd be put off if I knew about the cat. What else has he omitted to mention? What to do next? Ukrainian language seems very complex to me – a simple one or two word question seems to invite a very lengthy answer, sometimes even a whole paragraph! I'm thinking it must be as difficult for my potential guests. They are only trying to help.

Note: message Hanna tomorrow!!

CHAPTER 9
THE LANGUAGE BARRIER

THURSDAY, 9TH JUNE

Until now, we've only communicated by written messages in the group and I'm not sure Diana is understanding what I am saying and if I'm making myself clear with my responses to her.

I contact Hanna, a Ukrainian colleague of mine who lives in the UK, and she very kindly agrees to help with our conversation(s) via a joint video call later in the day.

I don't meet Diana's daughter on this occasion as Diana tells me she is sleeping and is a little scared about talking to me. I ask Diana if she is married, I think to reassure myself there won't be any additional surprise guests. She tells me she is divorced and had been living near her parents in Ukraine. Her parents have refused to leave as they own a smallholding in Kiev region and will not abandon their animals or their home. I ask if she knows if they are safe. (On reflection, what a thoughtless question!) She begins to cry and quickly follows with a "Sorry, sorry."

REFLECTION:

It's difficult to know what emotions are experienced when there are few words in common between us. Being a mum myself I appreciate she does not cry often for fear of upsetting or worrying her daughter and that she must be so resilient and strong to have got the three of them this far in their journey to safety. I'm the one who should apologise for being so thoughtless – how could she know if her parents are safe –nowhere is safe in Ukraine at the moment. How worrying for her.

This is a much better way to communicate. Although now I've 'met' Diana, I feel even more pressure on me to get them here. I really can't let them down now. Will I ever be able to work through the seemingly endless laws and regulations even more complex now with those relating to bringing an animal into the country? Where do I start?

CHAPTER 10
THE FAMILY LUNCH

SUNDAY, 12TH JUNE

Fortunately, the local authority support has been triggered by my application to the Government Ukrainian Sponsorship Scheme and I have been (to my relief) very speedily contacted by the local housing officer, saying they will need to carry out a home visit to assess the suitability and health and safety of my property (and I guess to assess my suitability and expectations about being a host).

I feel anxious about the visit as I know from my own experience as a home visitor that there are going to be concerns expressed about my spare bedroom, the size of which is, in my mind, shrinking by the minute. I have to think of a better plan.

I'm invited to lunch at my youngest daughter's house in the neighbouring village. My fifteen-year-old granddaughter is there, along with my daughter's partner's daughter, aged ten. It is a rare occasion for us all to sit round the table together, given that we are all busy and the girls lead a very active social life. I am pleased we are all together as it seems like a good time to tell them of my plans.

It appears to go reasonably well – my family are well used to my often knee-jerk reactivity and sometimes ill-thought-through ideas. After a few pertinent questions and assurances that I will be safe, I think they are fine with my idea. I do experience a brief flash of annoyance – albeit short lived – at the gentle suggestion that 'these refugees' might be criminals. I recognise and understand this sort of comment as microaggression and am usually comfortable challenging these views. However, it is more difficult to challenge family and friends, especially when they have my best interests at heart. Even though I am tempted to, it doesn't seem the right time.

I'm not prepared for my granddaughter's reaction though. She is, although open-minded in her attitude towards the plight of refugees – I'm so proud of her for that – unable to conceal her horror at the thought of my 'giving her room away to strangers' and asks sulkily, "Where will I sleep when I come to stay?"

I feel foolish – why didn't I think how she might have felt?

REFLECTION:

I wonder if I shall ever get a full night's sleep again. I feel so guilty about being such a terrible grandma.

CHAPTER 11
THE SOLUTION

MONDAY, 13TH JUNE

3 a.m. seems to be the time when I am often wide awake and also at my creative best. I've learned that it is a good idea to keep a notebook by my bed alongside my diary to jot down my ideas. Of course! Why didn't I think of this before? I will give up my garden office for my guests! Without a thought for the time – I'm convinced she spends half the night on her phone anyway as most teenagers do – I quickly tap out a message to my granddaughter:

> I've decided to offer my guests my office so you won't lose your bedroom at my house.

I sort of anticipate the adolescent 'Whatever' reply I receive – she must have been awake too. So, with a bit of quick grandma thinking, (I'm on a roll now) and not wanting to lose the moment, I follow up with,

> It will be better because I still get to spend time with you and that's the most important thing to me.

'Hearts' and 'love you' emojis are exchanged and our relationship is reclaimed.

At 12 feet x 15 feet, my garden room already houses two modern orange-covered double sofa beds. I had installed and furnished it to use as a therapy room/office space/training room just before the Covid lockdown struck. I love working in it and have made it my own, adding more bright colours: the two filing cabinets in pink and lime green; the pictures on the walls (close up shots of flowers from my garden) which I had enlarged and put onto canvas; and the two lamps, one like a big orange sun and the other a large blue glittery globe.

The small wooden summer house previously used as my therapy room had been re-sited at the bottom of my garden where my chickens free range. I intended to use it for my writing in the summer months; now it would need to be reused as my therapy room when clients visit in person, currently on two days a week.

There is a separate side entrance to my house, and a toilet, sink, washing machine, dryer and freezer in a small shed next to the garden room. My guests can share my kitchen and bathroom in the house. I look forward to buying the items I think might be useful to offer them as much independence – and us all as much privacy – as will be possible.

I check the Facebook page to see if others are asking questions or offering help and am surprised to notice a message from my neighbours, who have posted a question about hosting too.

REFLECTION:

I feel slightly more settled now with a more realistic plan in mind. I do worry whether my guests will be comfortable in their room and so happy that my granddaughter still loves me xxx.

I must pop round tomorrow to see my neighbours – I hope we can support each other. I don't feel quite so alone now it's all coming together. There is something magical about the power of thought – when you put out a call for guidance, albeit unconsciously, how it seems to be heard.

CHAPTER 12
THE TRAVEL ARRANGEMENTS

TUESDAY, 14TH JUNE

Nearly all of the arrangements are taking place via WhatsApp messages, with a few via email. Video calls between us will be useless without Hanna's support, given the language barrier. Hanna tells me about a translation app via Google, which hopefully will help if I can get my head around working it out – although I'm still not clear how this will work when making video calls.

Diana clearly seems to be managing very well from the messages we exchange, even though she tells me her English is not good. (I realise she is probably using the app at her end and is clearly more tech savvy than I am.) Even so, there are still several rather frustrating misunderstandings as not all messages translate well, even with the app, and I am struggling somewhat.

> **Diana**
> I don't know how long we will wait for the visa. Today I will go to the representatives of the mayor's office. I want to know if I can go to work here.

Trying to respond sympathetically and make sense of what she means while juggling the tasks of my normal full working day is not easy.

> **Me**
> I don't know what you mean – surely it's not worth you getting work there? Hopefully you will be here soon.

Due to my dyslexia, I'm used to making countless admin errors in both my personal and work life. In the past, these have been uncomfortable and sometimes financially costly, but mostly, I manage to resolve them eventually without too much damage. However, these arrangements are *so* important to get right. It is not just me at stake here, so I try to stay a little calmer and take more time – painstakingly and often obsessively checking and rechecking the paperwork.

I take an hour out from my work to visit my neighbours, and over a welcome coffee am delighted to hear that they are a little further on in the process with their guests – a mother and her seventeen-year-old son are due to arrive in a couple of weeks' time. It is helpful and reassuring to hear of their achievements in arranging the journey – which in their guests' case, was from Berlin. However, my neighbours seem exhausted, already having encountered a number of problems in securing their guests' permission to travel, and I am grateful when they kindly share some helpful tips about some of the pitfalls they have encountered and overcome.

Diana manages to upload the required letter which shows her and Alya's right to enter the UK, so I feel more confident that all – at least legally – is well. She's also sent a screen shot copy of their passports to reassure me. They are still awaiting their visas and Diana seems convinced from her messages that this is the biggest hold up. She seems unaware and quite dismissive when I tell her of the complexities and importance in ensuring an animal can be allowed to enter the UK. I appreciate her efforts to establish what else she needs to do her end and there have clearly been frequent visits to a vet in The Netherlands, which I'm imagining do not come cheaply. Apparently, the cat – poor thing – has been subject to several vaccinations, hopefully one of which is for rabies. Diana has sent me copies of the certificates to prove this, although it is difficult to know what they are for as they are written in Dutch – a language neither of us understand. There is still no sign of a pet licence – whatever that is? Again, it seems we have a problem with interpretation – this time between Dutch and Ukrainian languages at the vet. The only thing that is clear is that the cat has been microchipped, thus meeting a further requirement.

Although I am familiar with DEFRA[1] regulations relating to keeping my chickens, I have no idea about the rules for Ukrainian cats. I have visions of the cat being held in quarantine for months, or even of not being allowed to travel at all due to the risk of rabies. There is currently no rabies in the UK, the last case being identified more than a century ago, and I do not want to be the one responsible for bringing this terrible disease here – and am particularly concerned for my own pets' health and safety. I need to be careful I read and understand the paperwork from DEFRA properly.

There is much confusion regarding the pet licence v

pet passport – we are unsure if they have either or both of these – required for the cat to travel, and what needs to happen (if anything) once they arrive here regarding quarantine.

It is at this point that, thankfully, a DEFRA vet, Alina, contacts me. I explain the language difficulties and (amazing luck!) she speaks Russian, a language which is similar to Ukrainian and apparently easily understandable by Diana. I suggest including her in our WhatsApp group and I'm relieved when she agrees as I can keep track of her discussions with Diana and have more time to focus on preparing the room (at least mentally, as I'm still working in it).

Alina is extremely helpful in many other ways – above and beyond what I imagine is required of her. She confirms – after looking at the certificate – it is the pet passport that they already have. A blood test will be required thirty days later to ensure the rabies vaccine – Yay! Alina confirms the cat has had it! – has been effective. This thirty-day wait is a real blow. It seems that once we have sorted out one thing, another obstacle appears in our path. In addition to that, we learn it's unlikely that the cat will be allowed to travel by air and the other option is via ferry.

Alina pulls out all the stops to find out if the cat's blood test can be done once the cat has arrived at my house and it turns out it can – much to my potential guests' delight. I can almost hear them packing and half expect them to turn up on my doorstep the next day. I have to agree that I will prepare suitable accommodation to house the cat and ensure that she is kept in quarantine for the period required until the blood test has been taken and the results are clear. I will need a letter from DEFRA confirming my agreement to uphold the quarantine regulations.

Each time we face a new hurdle, I receive a *WHY?!'* from Diana. At least the ferry travel option is more convenient as there is a ferry port less than an hour's drive from me.

REFLECTION:

Feeling quite envious of my neighbours. They are a couple, and I'm negotiating this on my own. How will I manage?

I am starting to become uncomfortably aware of my own prejudice emerging, in that I am not acknowledging Diana's ability and intellect. I feel shame in my assumptions that attribute this to her culture and recognise some of my conjecture of her incompetence is really a projection of my own fears about mine driven by growing up with dyslexia that was never acknowledged. How much more will I learn about myself in this process?

I do feel for her though, and can see how hard she is working in what is a far from ideal situation and environment, and it must be quite costly for her too. She must feel confused and frustrated – and I do too.

Diana's messages don't help me to keep calm. Awoke from a horrible dream in which I was

33

frantically searching through websites, looking for a combination number to open a safe. Rosso had contracted rabies and the vet had taken him from me to lock him in the safe. I can totally understand that my potential guests are adamant they will not travel without their beloved pet; I feel bad about having to stick to the rules.

1 Department for Environment, Food and Rural Affairs

CHAPTER 13
THE HOME VISIT

THURSDAY, 16TH JUNE

The home visit is fortunately one element of the arrangements that does not pose any problems. I just need to attend to a couple of things, such as installing a particular type of carbon monoxide alarm, and I want to buy a dehumidifier to manage the condensation the additional 'bodies' might produce in the well-insulated space.

I am anxious to plan some time off work to get their room ready but don't want to do this until I know when they are coming. The thought of going back to using my old therapy room, which is now at the bottom of my two hundred foot plus garden, isn't particularly attractive. Although I don't anticipate there will be too many adjustments to make, and the more I think about it, the more it seems feasible – after all, it hopefully won't be long until my guests can find more permanent accommodation. My overall aim as I see it is to get them to the UK.

I will also need to get help with moving some of the

heavier furniture down the garden (such as my filing cabinet that contains client notes), work out what items could be left and used by my guests, and have some work done to the garden in order to make a path with stepping stones through the muddy chicken area for my clients to get to the therapy room. This will mean keeping my chickens locked in their shed on the days when clients visit in person as I'm aware not everyone shares my love of animals. Foggy, the magnificent white cockerel, can appear quite intimidating – although in reality, I only have to look at him and he struts off very rapidly down the garden, looking flustered and undignified. Rosso already goes to doggy day care on these 'in person' days so that will not be a problem.

I need to think about what else I will need to make a comfortable guest room. Under the 'Homes For Ukraine Scheme', I will receive £350 pro rata per month while my guests are with me, which is expected to be for a minimum of six months. After this, it is assumed they will have found their own place. From this expected payment, I buy a microwave, kettle and toaster, and a small slow cooker that I hope may be useful. I have been Googling 'What do Ukrainians like to eat?' Given that Diana says they are missing home cooked food, I thought they might like to make some stews and casseroles and their favourite dish, Borscht.[1]

I try to imagine I am going through a typical day and this helps me to think what they might need – although I realise this is making a huge assumption that their typical day is like mine.

There is some brief basic advice on the government website about possible requirements when guests first arrive and my neighbour is also helpful as she has already bought much for her guests' room. For more personal needs, I check with Diana and Alya which colours they prefer – it feels right to involve them and hopefully to help them feel at home as much as possible. I buy crockery and cutlery, a clothes rail and shoe rack, bedding, towels and a linen basket. I have a chest of drawers I don't use from my spare bedroom, a coat stand and a couple of folding chairs, a coolbox for milk and butter, extras such as a tray and bedside tables and lamps. As I am unsure of their tastes in both food and toiletries, I settle on a few basic food items and essentials like cleaning products.

I am warming – or is it resigned? – to the idea of welcoming their cat too and manage to find a spare litter tray, buy some cat litter, feeding bowls and just a couple of small packs of cat food to be going on with, knowing from experience that cats can be very fussy.

They are also to receive a little money from the council just after their arrival, so I am looking forward to taking them to shop for food and anything else I haven't thought of.

REFLECTION:

I love making a list, especially when it leads to a shopping trip or two.

It is surprising what we take for granted when everything we need for everyday use is at hand. Again, I am reminded how privileged I am. My lack of awareness of our cultural differences makes me a little nervous about buying for my guests and I recognise I am just thinking about this from my own perspective, which is all I can do before they arrive. I just hope I get most of it right.

Some friends are keen to offer their thoughts and ideas about what 'Ukrainians like/don't like' and their lifestyle generally. Much of this, of course, is based on sweeping assumptions which on the surface, seem positive, and based on their own preferences – the most common I've heard being, "All Eastern Europeans have a good work ethic." However, again I note I feel some unease with such comments. It will be interesting to see what it feels like if similar assumptions are made about me by my guests when they arrive.

1 Ukrainian soup dish – eaten hot or cold, mainly made with red beetroot and can include meat or fish.

CHAPTER 14
THE PRESSURE

TUESDAY, 21ST JUNE

The time passes quickly for me as we wait for the elusive visas. Mainly this is due to me being very busy in my daily work. I focus on making plans to rearrange my work schedule to fit around my new house guests' needs while hopefully maintaining our privacy. Unaware of what I am needing to arrange this end, I'm sure the wait must seem endless for my guests and Diana doesn't hold back from telling me this at every opportunity via her messages.

Their frustration is apparent as I try to interest them in their 'new home', sending photos of the room as it is before its makeover, and of my cats, dogs and chickens. They send me more photos of their cat. We continue to exchange messages several times a day. I ask what sort of work Diana might enjoy, what religion they are and if they would like me to find a church here they could attend. Diana seems to be getting more and more impatient (and I assume she must feel desperate) as many messages with exclamation marks and "What else do I need to do??", "I don't understand!!", "They (the authorities) are mocking me!" Although always polite and grateful for my efforts, it must be hard with the language barrier and cultural differences to understand the hold-ups.

I get the good news that Alya's visa arrived by email yesterday (she posts a screenshot of it), and today, Diana's. Now it seems all we have to do is discuss the last minute checks with Alina to ensure their cat can travel, set a date and book their ferry tickets! I will then be able to notify my clients of my intended week off work. Any gaps between my client appointments (usually reserved for writing notes) are filled instead with my plans for the 'great day' and the weekend before when I will clear out my room of all things 'office' and transform it into a more homely space for them.

It is even more challenging to stand my ground with my guests now their visas have arrived. It must be hard for them to see why they can't come straight away. I am determined to stick to the plan, although it is increasingly hard to say no. Another couple of days, in my mind, are worth the wait to avoid me being over stressed about completing my preparations and we can hopefully all relax when they get here.

REFLECTION:

I recognise my dreams are getting even more stress related – losing tickets, booking the wrong flight, being late for a job interview. I can see now why my neighbours are so tired. It's a little like getting everything done before going on holiday, except I'm not going on holiday, people are coming 'on holiday' to me and I get a feeling it's not going to be too restful. Even more apparent are our cultural differences and my guests' expectations of me – and indeed the UK in general. I can understand their haste to get here after everything they have been through. It's a real wake-up call for me when I consider, even with all our current escalating political problems, it is more desirable for them to be here than in their own dangerous homeland.

CHAPTER 15
THE TRAVEL ARRANGEMENTS

THURSDAY, JUNE 30TH

The Facebook group is a mine of information, especially when reading posts from hosts that are further along in the process, and I'm also enjoying having more chats than I've ever had with my neighbours, whose guests are arriving very shortly. It's good to get to know them better.

I take a pause over a coffee and my mind drifts to remembering my own chaotic arrival when moving here. It had been harrowing due to hitches with banks, solicitors and estate agents. Eventually, I arrived on a boiling hot day in August with chickens in boxes in the boot of a friend's car, my two cats in baskets and our cars packed to capacity with the clutter of random belongings in a futile attempt to assist the still absent removal van. My neighbours had been so welcoming, bringing out cold orange drinks. I can't imagine what went through their minds as we rolled up looking like the Beverley Hillbillies.

My musings are abruptly interrupted by Diana's message – now even more relentless in her need to get here. Alina maintains her professional obligations and calm, and continues to be kind and patient when communicating with us both, which helps me enormously.

Eventually, the cat – I understand she is called Luna – is finally granted official permission to travel. I also, following a quickly shared (with Alina) video scan around my guests' room, am provisionally granted permission to home Luna on the understanding that I take full responsibility in ensuring that she is kept in strict quarantine conditions until after we have received the blood test results. This means that on the journey from the ferry terminal to my house, I will not be allowed to stop the car, and that once here, Luna cannot leave their room, is preferably kept in a crate (which I will provide), and that I do not allow any other animals into the room. I am a little worried about taking this level of responsibility, knowing from my own experience how quickly cats can 'escape' through even the smallest of gaps, and my dog's and cats' natural curiosity and ability to 'sniff out' another cat seemingly within miles of my house.

So somewhat reluctantly, I quickly complete the forms which confirm my agreement, returning them to Alina, who assures me that another vet (who is based nearby) will take over the support in person when my guests arrive – the same one who will take the blood sample.

I explain in a message to Diana that I think a week the following Monday morning will be a good time to collect them as I will need the weekend before to finally clear out my 'office' and prepare their room. Not wanting to rush things at the last moment, I have to again hold my tongue as I ignore Diana's pleas to arrive on the Sunday.

It is still not possible to book the tickets until the

agreement about Luna's quarantine arrangements has been confirmed. Diana and Alya will need to plan their travel carefully – a three-hour train journey from where they are in The Netherlands and then a bus to the ferry terminal in Rotterdam ensuring they arrive in plenty of time to catch the overnight ferry. This will all add expense. I had a quick look at the ferry company website, and from what I can work out, it is going to be at least £300 for their tickets. I've never been entirely confident with booking travel tickets as my brain gets confused with the twenty-four-hour clock, and in this case, there will also be a time difference to contend with too. This needs to be a carefully coordinated arrangement that hopefully concludes with them arriving in the UK on the Monday morning when I plan to be free to collect them.

There follows a frantic forty-eight hours- I'm sure for Diana and Alya too. Working all day seeing clients – some online, some in person – glancing down at my phone and seeing messages popping up from Diana with more questions that I can't answer, although I try to respond in my breaks, usually reserved for note taking.

Alina messages me privately and confirms my agreement to abide by the quarantine regulations has been approved. She asks if there is anything else she can do to help. I ask if she would kindly book the ferry tickets – not wanting to encroach further on her time as I sense she is also busy, ours being just one of many of her 'cases'. I offer to send her the money if Diana transfers it to me rather than her having to arrange this with Diana directly. I am relieved when she accepts and really grateful she has taken this task from me.

My relief is short-lived, however, and my thoughts

return to the concern that Diana is fast running out of money. Knowing I can't afford to pay out this money and unable to ignore this any longer, not intending to offend her I pluck up the courage to ask Diana the question…

Her response is as I fear:

"I have very little (money) left. And the daughter wants that ice cream, that cake I can't refuse."

DIARY REFLECTION:

Wtf do I do now???

What if they miss the ferry? Where will they stay until the next one – does the ticket cover this? What if there is not a space on the next one? Is insurance included in the ticket price? I'm not sure I'm up to the job.

I ponder on what it is like for them preparing for another journey into an unknown country. What are they feeling?

Priority now, though, is to get their tickets.

CHAPTER 16
THE FACEBOOK FRIENDS

FRIDAY, JULY 1ST

I half-heartedly fire up my laptop, racking my brains to think about how we can overcome this latest problem. I decide to test out the power of social media – my best idea yet!

Here's what I posted:

> 'Dear Friends, It has been another long and testing week in attempts to negotiate licences, laws and visas for my lovely and desperate Ukrainian guests – a mum and her fourteen-year-old daughter and their cat – to get here. So now – so much out of my comfort zone – I'm asking for your help.
>
> My guests have run out of money, and unless you know otherwise, there is no financial support until they get here. They are currently in the Netherlands and need tickets from Rotterdam to Hull on the ferry.

46

According to Facebook, I have 290 friends. So could we test that theory, please, and ask you to send £1 each to my PayPal 'friends and family' account and I can pay for their ticket.

Thank you so much. I know we can do this.

Much 💜

REFLECTION:

I'm delighted my old skills from my fundraising days have not left me. From carol singing to sponsored walks and 'bucket of water challenges', I can be very persuasive when I see a need. Now let's see what happens.

CHAPTER 17
THE LAST LEG

MONDAY, JULY 4TH 2 P.M.

It is only 24 hours since my Facebook request and the donations are approaching £600! There are still more promised. I am unprepared for this overwhelming response. I can't believe it! Every time I see a notification come through, I feel moved to tears. Not just the £1 I'd asked for but £5! £10! £20! and more. People I've not seen for years are so generous – some, I know, can barely afford it themselves but still the donations keep coming. This means Diana and Alya can not only have the best cabin tickets, they can now buy meals on the ferry and even have a couple of treats on their journey. I'll forward any excess money to Diana when they arrive, to use for food, clothing or other essentials. They will have little luggage and must have left much behind in Ukraine.

Alina says she will try to book the tickets as soon as she can. I carry on working, keeping a watch on the group chat to see how things are progressing.

The rest of the day is a bit of a blur, but messages exchanged between us go something like this:

> **Alina**
> Alya's passport is out of date!

(Thirty-minute gap – I can sense my blood pressure going up)

> **Diana**
> His passe-partout is fine – we have letter with extension.

She posts screenshot of said letter.

> **Me**
> Phew!!

(Two-hour gap)
Screenshot of ferry tickets pop up on my screen.

> **Me**
> Thank you so much, Alina – I'll check them over when I get a minute.

(I check the tickets and can hardly believe it…blood pressure up. I check again)

> **Me**
> Alina, I think these are wrong – these are from Hull to Rotterdam!

> **Alina**
> Oh no – I'm so sorry. I don't have time to change them now. I have to take my children out straight after work. I'll do it tomorrow.

REFLECTION – 1 A.M.:

Alina seems very laid back about all this – then again, everyone is probably more laid back than me. What if there are no tickets left tomorrow? What if Diana and Alya are stranded in Rotterdam? What if…?

I have to resort to a glass of wine and one of the rather dubious sleeping pills I bought online, just to slow my racing mind.

CHAPTER 18
THE GOLDEN TICKETS

TUESDAY, 5TH JULY

All is well – tickets booked for arrival date of 11th July.

REFLECTION:

My mission is complete. My anxiety is replaced with excitement. I am thankful for the positive power of social media. At last I can relax into a fairly normal week until I start to transform my office into a guest room.

CHAPTER 19
THE BIG DAY

MONDAY, 11TH JULY 6 A.M.

Although tired from my weekend of preparing my guests' room, I'm still up early. The ferry is due in at 7.30 a.m., so of course, I am at the port in plenty of time. When I arrive, I am told by the port officials that I will have at least an hour's wait once the ferry has docked as the customs procedure will be lengthy. I busy myself with attempting to negotiate the tired looking drinks machine in the corner of the waiting area which eventually manages to splutter out a half-full paper cup of rather disgusting coffee. On my second attempt, I decide to go for the brown liquid which sort of resembles hot chocolate if I don't let it linger on my tongue for too long.

As I am replying to a long list of emails that have accumulated over the weekend – to try to distract me and calm my nerves– Diana sends a photo of herself with Alya in their cabin, saying excitedly,

"We are almost there and Alya is a little scared."

Around an hour later, seemingly the last passengers to

disembark, they emerge through the gates. They look confused and exhausted, although Diana still manages a smile. Their only luggage is in their two backpacks, with Alya carefully carrying Luna in a small cat carrier. We hug awkwardly and I try to explain with some rather strange sign language that we will not be able to stop on the journey home and ask if they wish to use the toilet before we leave. I'm hopelessly not making myself clear as they are already heading for the exit.

Our journey 'home' is uneventful, and somehow we luckily manage to miss the early morning rush hour traffic, which now seems to be stacking up on the other side of the carriageway. I'm finding it impossible to follow the conversation and try to ignore Diana is excitedly trying to tell me something via the translator on her phone. As we get within a mile of our village, I am slightly ashamed to feel grateful when she loses internet connection – our village is limited to one or two network providers and it seems she is not with either of them – so I can calm down a little and focus on my driving. I'm keen for them to see their room and a little nervous in case they don't like it.

REFLECTION:

Aware of feeling excluded as I wasn't able to join in with their conversation or make myself understood. It's quite disorientating being on my home ground and feeling so disadvantaged in my communication. I can only guess what it must feel like to them coming to this strange country. I'm not sure they would say if they weren't happy with anything. Part of me hopes they will, although I recognise that might raise in me my inability to make everything better. I can see this is going to be a busy and tiring week.

CHAPTER 20
THE FIRST 24 HOURS

MONDAY, 11TH JULY

All seems to be well with their room so far. It's still only 11a.m. so it seems like a good time to go shopping. I give them the remainder of the donations from my Facebook friends to buy toiletries or food that they would like and I am clear that we will mainly need to prepare our own meals due to my erratic working hours. Tonight, however, I'll prepare dinner – a safe ham salad? – and we will eat together in my kitchen.

The rest of the week will be taken up with visits from various departments of the council so it seems sensible to do their shopping now. At least I can relax when I know they have a few more home comforts and can rearrange their room the way they want it. I brace myself to tackle the 'big Tesco'.

I take a sunny yellow mug from the cupboard – it reminds me of sunshine, which I hope will cheer her – and make a coffee for Diana, taking it outside along with one for me, then place in on the garden table and wait for them to emerge from their room. Alya has some cans of cola she bought on the ferry.

It's already turning out to be a beautiful summer's day. The ground is parched and the bedding plants I have recently planted are looking a little thirsty. I must remember not to throw away the washing up water tonight to give them a drink. We are expecting the usual water restrictions this year so I try to be careful with every drop. I'm enjoying the peace and aware of a robin bravely sitting very close to my shoulder. I remember a favourite aunt of mine who used to say seeing a robin is a symbol of a new beginning.

Diana comes out, sits down beside me and takes a sip of coffee. I notice she flinches a little and I'm wondering if it may not be to her taste but she is too polite to say.

"Would you like to make a list?" I ask her via the translator with a few hand gestures thrown in.

Diana looks confused.

Alya joins us, and having overheard my question exclaims, "OH YES! SHOPPING!" She laughs. "Mum doesn't make lists." She clearly understands my English and my gesticulations better than her mum.

In Tesco car park, I sense we are in for an interesting experience as I get out of the car and they rush past me and into the store as if they have won a trolley dash prize. I stand alone with my car boot open, disappointed I can't share with them my bright idea of bringing the cool box in my car boot.

Once inside, I scan around the vast shop in the hope of finding them, feeling slightly anxious as I sometimes did when my children were small and I lost sight of them for a few minutes. Then I spot them in one of the beauty aisles, Alya lovingly stroking a bottle of shampoo against her chest as if it was a baby. She is clearly thrilled with her find. I spot Diana in another aisle looking for something, although I'm not quite sure what, and she mumbles something about sausage as I approach.

I realise I am feeling unnecessarily over protective as I want to help them find the best priced items and I probably don't do a very good job of holding back to avoid spoiling their pleasure in finding some of the things they have been deprived of since they left Ukraine. There is much that they can't find and I feel helpless as I try to help by offering some sort of guidance as to where everything is located and what might be best value, but in the end, I give up and allow them to enjoy the freedom of searching for what they need.

After an hour and a half of this frantic spending spree, I'm exhausted and with my head buzzing, I'm just looking around for a chair to sit on by the underwear department when Diana also succumbs and indicates she wants to go home. She has a headache and I guess the stress of the journey and the last few weeks has caught up with her. I don't need asking twice and we load up the car with their variety of goods (ignoring my offer of the coolbox) and we drive home a lot faster than I drove there.

When we arrive back home, I help them offload all the shopping. They look mystified when I present them with the coolbox. I am quite concerned as I note they have not left Luna in the crate I have provided and she is roaming freely around their room, eventually scurrying under the bed. My attempted suggestion that she needs to be contained more safely is not heard and I decide to leave it for today as we are all clearly worn out. I go to collect Rosso from daycare.

When he sees my guests in the garden, I think he is never going to stop jumping up at them. All the efforts I have put in to try to train him to greet people calmly are wasted as Alya strokes him vigorously and makes such a fuss of him – he loves it!

We eat dinner, I wash up, and at around 10 p.m., finally sit down and put my feet up, feeling quite proud they are here and all seems to have gone reasonably well. I'm just dozing off in the chair when I hear the back door open. Rosso barks and I hear the shower in the downstairs bathroom running. This goes on for at least half an hour and I want to go to bed but I can't as I'll need to lock the door for the night.

I wait until all is quiet then thankfully, I go up to bed, feeling the need to lock my bedroom door – although I'm not quite sure why.

REFLECTION:

Well, that was a little different to my normally well organised shopping trip! I'm getting used to the translator app – and dreading it at the same time as it takes much energy on all our parts. At least now we can communicate verbally as well as with texts, although there are still some words that don't quite convert. I couldn't understand why they laughed when I said, "You won't need to buy eggs as I have a good supply from my chickens." This caused much laughter until I realised 'eggs' translated into testicles!

Addressing the uncomfortable issue of them not keeping Luna in the crate seems a bit mean. Today was OK with Rosso in day care but I dread to think what might happen if he gets into their room before Luna is out of quarantine. How do I stress the importance of this to Diana and Alya? I will need to make some ground rules – maybe a good idea to let them know the back door will be locked at 10 p.m. and ask them to be careful with their use of water? I feel a slight discomfort at having people around and unsure about imposing these 'rules.' I guess I'll get used to it – I don't have much choice now.

CHAPTER 21
THE ADMIN DELUGE

TUESDAY, 12TH JULY

There is so much to do and the local authority with their various departments are very supportive and accessible. The visit today is to give us some information on how to apply for a UK bank account for Diana. She will need one in order to pay in a salary when she is working, as well as Child Benefit and the elusive Burp, which they will need if they decide to stay in the UK for longer than six months.

Carol, the council housing worker, talks Diana through the Universal Credit application she is making on her behalf. She brings the small one-off payment for Diana and Alya and takes the details needed to apply for a National Insurance number – important for work, although Diana can still legally get a job in the meantime for the first six months she is here. I assist with the translation using my phone, as their network still does not receive a good signal – although Carol says there may be a free sim card available with access to a better network.

Then Carol wants to see Diana and Alya on their own

– I assume to check they are happy to stay with me and that I am not taking advantage of them in any way. I leave them to it and go back to the house. Carol eventually follows me and asks if I am experiencing any problems. We talk about the challenges with the language and agree this hopefully won't be insurmountable so I decide to bide my time and see how things go. She tells me there may be access to English lessons for Diana, and Alya's English will hopefully improve further when she gets a school place after the summer holidays. She confides in me that some hosts have struggled with the challenges of hosting for various reasons.

We arrange another visit from a different council department to explore the possibility of Alya's schooling. I hope she may be able to get a place at my granddaughter's school. Carol suggests I call them. We agree that any messages sent to Diana will be copied to me to avoid any misunderstandings.

I go to pick up a form from my G.P. surgery in the village and arrange to meet with Diana at 5 p.m. in my kitchen to complete it and all the online forms that seem to be accumulating. The G.P. receptionist is not very helpful – I think she is new – and insists Diana will need an NHS number before she can register with the G.P. I'm not sure if she's right and I do sense a slight discriminatory tone in her voice so I decide to check with Carol rather than arguing. It is too late to call the school now so I add it to my list to do tomorrow.

I knock on their door at 5.30 p.m., as Diana had not come to my house at 5 p.m. as agreed. Rosso is right behind me and immediately senses the cat in the room. A sleepy Diana eventually answers the door, apologising profusely.

"I am so tired. Can we do it tomorrow?"

Before I can answer, Rosso charges into the room, somehow squeezing between my legs, which are pressed tightly together to hopefully avoid this disaster. In a few seconds, he manages to devour Luna's food and chase her under the bed. Alya emerges and tries to lure Luna out. I hear the cat spitting and hissing from her hiding place.

Rosso comes back to me, looking for approval. I hold tightly onto his collar, and trying to be understanding, say, "Of course, no problem." Alya is trying to tell me something about Luna, I think, but I can't be sure and haven't got the energy to find out. I return to my house, pulling a disappointed Rosso by his collar behind me.

REFLECTION:

There is so much incomplete admin already stacking up and I am keen to deal with as much as possible before I go back to work next week. Everything takes at least twice as long when running through a translator, especially one that doesn't always work properly! I have nothing left today! Have my guests eaten a proper meal? All I could see in their room were a couple of bowls of half-eaten cereal and they didn't come into the kitchen to cook. If I don't stop getting so worried about them, I'll not survive the week. I'm wondering what the challenges were for other hosts and count myself lucky that I've not encountered any serious problems so far.

CHAPTER 22
THE AMAZON

WEDNESDAY, 13TH JULY

Carol visits again, bringing a new sim card – donated free by the network company – for Diana's mobile phone. It is a great gesture but Diana's delight quickly turns to disappointment when I say that, unfortunately, it will be no use around here as it is not from one of the two providers that offer decent coverage in this village.

Alya interrupts me to explain, "Luna will not use her cat litter tray. She doesn't like the cat litter!"

I resist the temptation to say, "She doesn't have to like it – just shit in it," but before I can formulate a more polite reply, Diana is waving her phone at me to show me a link to Amazon shopping.

"Can we order some things tonight when you are free, please?"

I add this to my ever-increasing list of 'things to do this evening after dinner'.

I'm just reluctantly toying with the idea that we might need to go shopping again this afternoon (it is already 2 p.m.) when Julie, another council worker arrives to discuss the school options. I still haven't got around to calling the school and I'm grateful when Julie says she will do it. She also leaves a sheet with measuring instructions for a school uniform for Alya, most of which will thankfully be supplied free of charge as I imagine with all the hidden costs and extras we haven't accounted for their money will run out quickly until Diana can get work, which I can tell she is keen to do. I hunt around for a tape measure for Diana to measure Alya and manage to find one that starts at 3 inches, having only partially been chewed by Rosso.

As Diana gets to work on the measurements, I look online for a local bus timetable – it will be good for them to start to get around independently and I'll not be so free to drive them around next week when I'm back at work.

At 5 p.m., Diana comes into my kitchen clutching the small slow cooker I bought.

"What is this thing?? It takes sooo long."

I try to explain and feel a little irritated, assuming she is not appreciative of my thoughtfulness. Then I realise that of course she has no idea what the point of it is. Why would she? I take it from her and put it at the back of the kitchen cupboard I'm sure I'll find a use for it. I reach for the yellow mug and make a coffee for Diana.

We sit down at the kitchen table with my laptop and begin the long task of applying for the bank account, Child Benefit and the Burp. None of the websites have any option to apply in Ukrainian so it is a very slow process to establish the correct information from Diana, input it and then first identify and then upload any required documents, all of which are somewhere in the depths of Diana's mobile phone. We are finding it really difficult to know which documents are required as they are mainly written in Ukrainian.

It's 9.30 p.m. and we have only just completed the Child Benefit and bank account application. As we are trying to work out what is needed for the Burp, Diana shows me a text message with a "What is this?" I see it explains she has an appointment in town tomorrow at 9 a.m. to continue her application for Universal Credit. I have a dental appointment myself so I can't take her. This seems an ideal time to introduce the bus timetable so I send a copy to her phone and we give up for the evening with a promise to resume our efforts tomorrow.

DIARY REFLECTION:

I need to call my phone network provider and put on my best begging voice to see if they will offer any special rates for my guests so they can use their phones more reliably when away from here.

We didn't have time to set up an Amazon account so I have offered to order from my account if they need anything in the meantime. Worried, as I'm trying to ensure they are secure financially and won't need to rely on me and I get the feeling Diana feels the same. I can't imagine what it must be like to be so far away from parents/grandparents and all their home comforts though, so again I hold back from telling them my concerns. Diana is constantly in touch with them by phone – earpods permanently in her ears – pleased I've got unlimited data in my house. I imagine she is keen to send them money as the situation in Ukraine is dire, with many power cuts, lack of food in the shops and no heating as the country's infrastructure gradually gets destroyed.

I feel frustrated at my lack of ability to ease their situation and that I can't manage their expectations of being in the UK. Much of this frustration emerges when Diana and Alya seem to question everything I do to try to help with a "Why (is this needed)?" or "Why can't we get a phone signal?" They are understandably comparing it with their memory of how things were (seemingly) better in Ukraine.

I recognise this is reflective of my own frustrations at our government, who seem to be oblivious that we are heading for further crisis in the NHS and indeed generally with much unrest fuelled by lack of leadership. There are some posts on social media which really rile me when they refer to this problem as made worse by 'the refugees!' I try to ignore them but it's hard not to respond angrily. Instead, I've deleted several 'friends' because of their judgemental comments – sadly, the negative side of social media.

CHAPTER 23
THE ANGER

THURSDAY, 14TH JULY

I am awoken at 7.30 a.m. by my video doorbell camera ringing to register activity at the side gate, along with Rosso's loud reminder just in case I haven't heard what I imagine he believes are all the intruders coming to attack me. (He even reacts like this to a doorbell on television!) I look out of the bedroom window to see Diana and Alya running towards the bus stop!

It seems I may have the morning to myself, so after a rare uninterrupted leisurely breakfast, I brace myself for the call to my phone network providers. As I'm in full swing, praising them for their exemplary service to my account so far, I see a text message come through from Carol.

'There is a possible job vacancy that Diana may be interested in…'

I'm clearly getting nowhere with the phone network, who tell me they "couldn't possibly offer any discount for refugees." I loudly express my disappointment with them, have a brief rant about the huge profits they make, and before ending the call abruptly, threaten half-heartedly to take my custom elsewhere. Knowing I won't as that will leave me without service too, I let it go and calm myself a little to call the number that Carol has sent – a local potato supplier. It is a small established family business around three miles from here.

I'm lucky to be able to speak to the owner, who is keen to help and offer Diana a job which involves sorting and grading potatoes – with the provision that she can speak English well enough to be safe in the workplace. This feels a much more friendly and welcoming conversation than the one with the phone company and he offers her a 'hands on' interview tomorrow morning. He is concerned about her legal right to work in the UK without a NI number and I feel quite knowledgeable for a change when I explain the situation and how he might be reassured from the Home Office letter she has to verify what I am saying and that she is able to work prior to the number arriving.

Around 10 a.m., the doorbell sets Rosso off barking again. I go outside to see an Amazon parcel left by the gate. I don't recall ordering anything this week and then surprisingly notice it's not addressed to me but to Diana! I'm so pleased she has managed to get an account set up – already more independent, which I hope will help them to feel more settled.

At my dental appointment, I try to register Diana and Alya as patients and book them a check-up. I am shocked by the receptionist's response when I say I want to register my Ukrainian guests.

"How many are there?" she asks tiredly, "One, two, ten?"

Now I'm feeling angry (probably partly left over from my earlier conversation with the phone company) and don't hold back in my response.

"Do you realise how rude that sounds? They are human beings, not a herd of cattle!"

She is embarrassed and apologises, although she clearly doesn't understand why I respond like this. I snatch the two forms she hands me and leave the surgery, trying to slam the door behind me for additional impact but it has a stopper on it so I can't.

When I get home from the dentist, my mood is not helped when I open the two letters I find on the mat. The first is my tax bill, substantially more than I was expecting. The second I have to read two or three times before it sinks in. A speeding fine dated 11th July – caught on camera on the journey home when I collected Diana and Alya from the ferry terminal!

REFLECTION:

Not quite the quiet day I was hoping for. Why does everything seem so challenging? How on earth did Diana manage to get signed up with and order from Amazon in less than 24 hours?? I realise I'm going to have to have more confidence in her abilities to work things out for herself. I'm so impressed they felt able to take themselves off to town on the bus and recognise I underestimated them both. I hope Diana's interview goes well. Trying not to interfere too much and focus on planning my birthday weekend.

CHAPTER 24
THE INTERVIEW

FRIDAY, 15TH JULY

It is my birthday. We are all up early. I take Diana to the interview. She is clearly as concerned as I am about her ability to understand English and the fact that she will not be allowed to use her phone to translate in a factory environment, even if she can get a signal – which is unlikely given the rural location of the workplace.

I try to help her prepare on our short car journey, offering an introduction in English.

"Hello, my name is Diana. I have come for an interview."

We laugh nervously as she repeats this several times until we feel confident she can be understood. I drop her off and arrange to collect her in an hour. I am in awe of her courage facing this on her own and cross my fingers hoping she is offered the job.

She is smiling when I collect her and it sounds like it went well. Another staff member who, although speaks Polish (which is very different to Ukrainian), is also able to understand a little Russian too, so the manager will put them together initially if he decides to offer her the job. He will let us know next week, he tells us, taking my number.

Diana seems pleased when we arrive home. I make her a coffee in the yellow mug and we sit and chat via the translator, soaking up the beautiful sunshine in my garden.

"How will I get to work if I get the job?"

I have to admit I haven't thought of that. There is no bus travelling in that direction and I won't be able to guarantee giving Diana a lift as I will be working myself.

REFLECTION:

I've held out high hopes for getting Diana settled in work as soon as possible. She is saying she might not be able to get there under her own steam. I was a single parent holding down three jobs at one point and walking two miles to the launderette with a bag of washing. Then I feel bad for judging her after all she has been through – is still going through. At least I was not in an unfamiliar country. Although she is a relatively young woman, the traumas of war must have taken their toll on her health – both mental and physical.

Today's Amazon parcel – a new litter tray for Luna.

CHAPTER 25
THE PARTY

SATURDAY, 16TH JULY

Today is turning out to be another gloriously sunny one. I open up the big gates between me and my neighbour's house and all are invited to my party, along with a few relatives and friends.

Diana is in my kitchen making a huge pan of borscht for us to try. The men take over the BBQ with the usual light hearted (although I suspect competitive) banter as to who knows the best way to maintain the right temperature to cook with. I struggle with the technicalities of the music speaker volume – first too quiet and then too loud, although it doesn't matter as my neighbours are here so they won't be upset by it!

Diana, Alya and my neighbour's guests (Josyp and his mother, Nadiya) talk freely in Ukrainian – a welcome break for them, I imagine.

It's all very easy and relaxed and we have a dance and a laugh. The men are fooling around and dancing together. Diana and some of my guests stay up chatting in the garden long after I am in bed.

REFLECTION:

Good to see they seem a little more settled and getting on with their 'neighbours'. What a lovely day!

CHAPTER 26

THE SIMILARITIES AND THE DIFFERENCES

SUNDAY, 17TH JULY

We are having a restful day. I'm pottering about (my favourite expression), tidying up after the party. I cook breakfast for my stepson, who stayed over. I'm enjoying catching up with him and all his news as I don't see him very often.

When he goes home, I notice Diana is sitting in the garden. She is on her phone and looks like she is crying. I make a coffee in the yellow mug, take it out to her and place it on the table beside her, feeling concerned that something awful has happened.

Unable to make out what she is saying to the caller on the other end, I sit quietly, soaking up the lunchtime sun, wait until she has finished her call and then ask her, "What's wrong?"

She tells me her friend's son is seriously ill in hospital and she is very worried about him and can do nothing to help from here. There are continual attacks every night on the village in Ukraine, very near to where her parents are living, and this is another constant source of worry for her. She quickly dries her tears again, showing her resilience in resisting showing her feelings, and especially not to worry Alya.

I feel helpless so I change the subject and ask her about Ukraine before the onset of the war. I'm curious to know if there is a social class system and if women are treated equally there. I ask about her relationships, Alya's father, her parents... we seem to have much in common around past relationships and both being only children of older parents.

Our conversation drifts to the party and I say, "Wasn't it funny watching the men dancing last night?"

Diana looks surprised, and although it could be that she doesn't understand, I have a sense she is not comfortable about this. Beginning to feel uneasy myself, I ask a direct question to clarify.

"How do you view homosexuality in Ukraine?"

This very clearly now disturbs her. "It is a sin!" she shouts. "It says so in the Bible."

Shocked at her views, I get up and walk into the house, making some excuse about going to the bathroom. Taking her untouched yellow mug of coffee, I throw it angrily into the sink.

We barely speak the rest of the day – I'm aware I'm avoiding her.

In the evening, I see her through the kitchen window in the garden using the hose to water a couple of bedding plants. Earpods in, she is speaking very quickly in Ukrainian on her phone again. It feels like a good time to try to make my peace. Pouring two glasses of Malbec from the bottle left over from the party, I go out to the garden.

(Trying to ignore as I pass, the three small items of clothing she has pegged out on the washing line – feeling this is yet another waste of our currently precious water. I need to stay calm for this next bit.)

I offer her a glass of wine, saying, "You prefer this to my coffee?"

She smiles. I think that's a 'yes'!

I move on to what I'm afraid of discussing. "I hope you are ok? I am finding this really difficult to say and I don't want you to be upset but I feel I have to say it. I find your views on homosexuality offensive."

Diana responds by quoting lengthy passages from the Bible, rapidly tapping them into the translator as she aims to cement her beliefs. At this moment, Alya joins us. Clearly hearing the gist of the conversation, she looks nervously at me and then her mum.

For her sake, I reply with, "Then we must decide to hold our different views."

Diana nods in agreement.

REFLECTION:

I realise that we all have our own opinions and beliefs, and Diana's views on homosexuality are not necessarily the same as everyone in her homeland. At least she is brave enough to speak her mind and hold true to her beliefs. I hated her borscht, it was too salty for me, although I wasn't honest enough to say so! I suspect she hates my coffee but she does not want to appear ungrateful. So the yellow mug is replaced by a wine glass and peace reigns in our home.

CHAPTER 27
THE BICYCLE

MONDAY, 18TH JULY

The fun of the party already seems far behind us and for me it's back to work tomorrow.

Today will be a frantic tying up of as many loose ends as I can. Any further form filling, managing visits from the council and supporting my guests in becoming more settled will have to fit around my client work from now on. In the main, I hope the processes to apply for Child Benefit is completed, or at least out of my hands and submitted for approval.

We receive a message to say Diana has got the job! 8 a.m. – 4 p.m. Monday to Friday. She also starts work tomorrow – Perfect!

I see a message on Facebook – aside from my neighbours, it is becoming my go-to place to connect with other hosts – from someone (Linda) offering not one but two bicycles free of charge to Ukrainian guests. I contact her immediately and we arrange to go and see them that evening. They were bought for the Linda's guest who left rather suddenly, having gone to stay with relatives and work down South somewhere. She is happy to let us have them on the understanding that when they are no longer needed, they will be passed on to other Ukrainian guests.

Diana is delighted, immediately jumps on the bike and speeds off down the road to try it for size. She is gone for some time and I wonder if she is OK. When she eventually returns, she indicates the seat needs adjusting – she is very tall – and she easily does this herself with a spanner lent by Linda. I suggest the other bike goes to my neighbour's guest if she wants it as it is too big for Alya – who will not need it anyway as when she starts school she can go on the bus.

I agree to take Diana to work tomorrow if Linda's husband cannot deliver her bike by then – and in any case, we clearly won't be able to get to the shops to buy a pump, lights and helmet for the bike until tomorrow evening after work anyway.

I am shocked when Diana says she has no need to wear a helmet, and all my concerns and gruesome examples of how dangerous it will be fall on deaf ears. I look at Linda, who rolls her eyes upwards and shrugs. She tells me she has already experienced from her own guest's speedy departure to another part of the UK that it seems Ukrainian women, once they have made their mind up, can be very obstinate. I'm not sure I agree with this generalisation but I don't challenge it. On this occasion, I feel I have an ally who would back up my concerns.

As we are chatting, Linda's husband comes out and without making any fuss, pops Diana's bike in the back of his large van. He follows us home and deposits it at my house with a promise to deliver the other bike tomorrow, when I have asked my neighbour's guest if she would like it. This means I won't have to take Diana to work in the morning and I can start at least one day in a calm and organised way.

REFLECTION:

The kindness and generosity of people never ceases to amaze me.

In my mixed-up dreams, I see Diana flying through the air having been thrown from her bike at that really dangerous crossroads and picture Alya being left as an orphan living with me. It is hard to accept Diana's choice not to wear a helmet and I can't help feeling responsible for her safety. I realise I need to 'let go' a little as I become even more aware of the realities of the differences between us and hope I can learn to accept them without compromising my own beliefs.

CHAPTER 28
THE LIE-IN
(THAT ISN'T)

TUESDAY, 19TH JULY

Awaking from a half-decent sleep, I am enjoying my last few precious minutes in bed before I return to my full-on day back at work. I snuggle down a bit, feeling really proud of how much we have achieved in a week since my guests arrived, with only a slight unease in the hope Diana gets to work safely.

As I feel Rosso snuggle at my feet, we both yawn and stretch and I glance at the clock by my bed. 7.30 a.m.! I gradually become aware that neither of us had heard the video doorbell sensor alarm to indicate Diana had left for work. Surely I remembered to charge the doorbell batteries … PING! I glance at my phone on the bedside table.

Message from Diana:

WE HAVE A PROBLEM!

I drag myself out of bed, Rosso sighs. I go to the spare

83

bedroom (at the back of the house) and look out of the window. Diana is in the yard, pacing up and down, phone in hand, every now and again pausing to look sorrowfully at her new bike.

She sees me at the window and I can hear her even through the double glazing.

"IT IS DEAD!" she almost screams at me, raising her eyes and hands upwards as if she thinks someone in the cloudless blue sky can help her.

Grumpily pulling on the nearest clothes I can find – my gardening trousers, T-shirt and slippers – I go downstairs and out into the garden. As I get closer, I see the bike is indeed 'dead'– well, at least one of its tyres is. I manage to somehow resist saying, "I knew we should have got a pump (along with a helmet) before you used the bike," although I want to, and I beckon her to help me to open the big gates to see if my neighbours are up yet. I'm certain they'll have a pump as Tony is an avid cyclist. They are not – up, that is – although I manage to disturb the neighbours the other side (or rather Rosso does by barking and waking their dog.)

Margaret – other dog's mother – comes out in her nightie and heads for her shed to look for a pump. "I'm sure I've seen one in there somewhere…" she mutters as we venture optimistically into the dark and dusty Aladdin's cave.

We search for a few minutes, shifting three bike frames, a couple of folded pasting tables and several assorted garden chairs from one side to the other – but no pump. I thank Margaret, try to untangle the cobwebs from the roof of the shed that have accumulated in my already messy morning hair and emerge into the light. I think the whole street must be awake by now with all the barking dogs, so after huffing a bit, I grab my car keys, shoo Diana into my car as if she is a chicken, and take her to work. After all, I can't be responsible for her being late on her first day, can I?

She will need picking up at 4 p.m. so I try to explain I don't finish work until then and will be a bit late. I leave her at the gates of the potato farm looking a bit lost, feeling mean for my grumpiness now – she is clearly nervous.

I return home to three Amazon parcels for Diana. I leave them on Diana's bed in their room where Alya is still asleep, clearly not disturbed by the commotion earlier today – typical teenager!

I feed Rosso and take him to doggie day care. I get ready to welcome my first client of the day, already feeling like I've had no time off at all.

Just after 4 p.m., I collect Diana. She seems happier, although she is clearly exhausted. I think her day has gone well. All the way home, she speaks constantly in Ukrainian into the translator on her phone, punctuated with an English 'WHY'? every time she loses the signal.

My day has gone well too, after the unwelcome start, and my neighbour Tony has kindly found a pump and inflated the bike tyre ready for tomorrow.

It turns out Diana's manager is keen to see the Burp and it is the only form we have not managed to complete so far. After my dinner, I tap on the door of their room – no answer. I see through the open blinds that Diana is asleep on the bed. It will have to wait until another day.

REFLECTION :

I'm quite getting used to these dramatic outbursts. How different to our often subdued British reactions where we don't really show our feelings.

CHAPTER 29

THE RELUCTANT BLOOD DONOR

WEDNESDAY, 27TH JULY

The familiar and melodious doorbell followed by the click of the front gate tells me Diana has gone to work. I'm feeling quite relaxed as I start work this morning. It seems we have settled into a routine and I'm not needed quite so frequently as I was when my guests first arrived.

However, today is a big day for Luna – in fact, for all of us. A DEFRA vet is visiting when Diana returns from work, to take Luna's blood sample and to see if everything is going smoothly and that I am keeping to the quarantine regulations. I'm slightly uneasy about her visit as I'm aware that although Luna remains in their room – "She's not an outdoor cat," Alya tells me – I know they are not keeping her in the crate as we agreed. This puts me somewhat on edge due to the previous Rosso 'incident'. He is now very aware there is a CAT! who hopefully might be up for a chase when my two cats are 'not available' to satisfy his enjoyable exercise routine.

I know that taking a blood sample from a cat can be

quite challenging and a traumatic experience for the cat, and if the vet is unable to get the sample, Luna may have to be quarantined elsewhere for several months. I imagine Diana and Alya are not looking forward to the procedure either – no-one, especially these clearly animal loving Ukrainians, like to see animals in discomfort.

Around 5.15 p.m. Rosso barks forcefully – a slightly different bark to his usual greeting alert and not a particularly welcoming one. Maybe he can sense it is a vet, and from what I can see through the side window of my kitchen, a very serious looking one at that. Carrying a huge black case, she clearly means business. I let him out into the garden while I greet her – keen to make a good impression in the hope she will be understanding of my minor deviations from the quarantine regulations which I see as beyond my control.

As I walk with her to Diana and Alya's room, there is a scuffle followed by screams of laughter from Diana and Alya, and Rosso is hurtling down the garden with Luna in close pursuit. This is not a good start!

Alya manages to retrieve Luna, who looks really pleased with herself at asserting her right to live here and does not seem too bothered about her failed escape attempt. I hardly dare look at the vet, who is looking even sterner than when she arrived, so I busy myself with helping to lure Luna out from where she has returned to – her favourite hiding place under the bed in the far corner of the room. This serves to distract the vet from dwelling on the 'incident' and she turns out to be kind, firm and extremely skilful in extracting the blood sample.

On the whole, after the rocky start, all goes well and the vet leaves with a good sample of Luna's blood and the promise of a phone call as soon as she gets the hopefully all clear result.

We all breathe out.

Alya says, "I would like to train to be a vet when I leave school but don't think I will be clever enough."

This reminds me we haven't heard about the school yet.

REFLECTION:

Yet again I'm reminded of the differences in the way we prioritise things. I found myself getting a little irritated when Diana and Alya laughed at Luna's escape as they seemed oblivious to the possible implications. Our passion and love for animals, especially our beloved pets, is obvious. However, when we don't agree on the importance of upholding the quarantine laws, I find myself feeling superior and that sits uncomfortably with me too.

CHAPTER 30
THE BURP!

TUESDAY, 2ND AUGUST

My morning message from Diana reads:

> Hello, I want to ask you if you will have time and opportunity tomorrow to help me fill out the form? Because today I just don't have the strength, and there is a lot of writing here...

Her English is improving – she is taking online lessons – and I am getting used to interpreting her words so I'm aware she means 'tonight' not 'tomorrow' and I also know she means the form to apply for the Burp (residency permit). A task, having looked at the application process on the website, I've tried to push to the back of my mind – and one I have been dreading.

However, it has to be done.

> Of course

I reply.

7 o'clock after dinner?

Diana knocks on the back door and comes in just after 7 p.m. She is looking exhausted as always and is rubbing her left lower back with a pained expression.

"Coffee?" I ask with a smile, pointing to the cupboard where I keep it.

She raises her eyebrows and before she can respond further, I take two wine glasses from the cupboard and am searching for the corkscrew to open a rather nice bottle of Malbec. She indicates a half inch measure with her thumb and forefinger although I pour us both a good half glass full. I think we will need it.

Two hours later we manage to establish that an appointment needs to be made in Sheffield – the nearest office – which is over an hour's car journey away. Diana appears unphased by this and looks on her phone at a UK map to find Sheffield. I'm vaguely aware she has mentioned the city before but can't quite remember why. She and Alya will need to take their passports there and get their fingerprints digitally taken as evidence of their identity. Once the Burps are processed, they will need to make a second journey to collect them.

Every step of the way, as I plough through the seemingly endless documentation, I have to explain to Diana what I am doing and ask questions about information needed from her. This mainly entails her scrolling up and down, searching through emails on her phone, copying and pasting into the translator and me finally checking with her before I input it to the online forms.

I tell her I will not be able to commit to taking them to

Sheffield and suggest they could go on the train – although I am concerned because there are currently many cancellations on that route. I have visions of them being stranded somewhere and me trying to find them and being charged for the missed or cancelled appointment – and they still won't have their very important Burp!

We finally manage to secure the first available appointment on a Saturday a few weeks away and hope that their passports are back in time as we had to send them off when we applied for the Child Benefit (which still has not been finalised).

We eventually give up for the evening, tired but relieved, having almost achieved one of the final hurdles to secure their residency.

REFLECTION:

I note with alarm that the bottle of Malbec is empty. I'm certain I'm responsible mostly. Thirsty business this form filling.

CHAPTER 31

THE DOCTOR'S APPOINTMENT

THURSDAY, 4TH AUGUST

Diana doesn't go to work today.

She tells me, "My back is bad; I need to see a specialist."

At first, I think she means a consultant. I'm thinking, 'You'll be lucky to see any sort of doctor in the next few weeks, let alone a specialist.' We persevere with the translator and after much effort, it turns out she had been seen by a chiropractor in Ukraine last year who told her she needed an injection. I'm hoping it is nothing serious and I'm concerned that she will lose her job if she takes much time off work as she has not been there long. I think the way she is describing her symptoms, it is nothing more than back strain, probably due to her recently starting manual work and all the cycling. So I suggest I try to make an appointment with the G.P. here in the village – where I had eventually managed to get her and Alya registered without an NHS number. (Previous receptionist – 0, Me –

1). I'm holding on to the hope the G.P. can reassure her that this is nothing serious.

"Today?" she asks.

"Unlikely," I reply under my breath. "It's hardly an emergency."

I try to ignore her puzzled "WHY?" I'm already anticipating a battle to get an appointment at all, let alone one in the near future.

Waiting 'on hold' on the phone to the surgery for 45 minutes gives me an opportunity to prepare in my mind my imploring speech for the doctor's receptionist to secure an appointment for today so Diana won't need to take more time off work. When I eventually get through, I explain that I will need to accompany Diana to help her translate and I'm only available today. Amazingly, we are granted an appointment for this evening. I'm delighted, even though Diana doesn't seem to share my enthusiasm.

As we walk down to the surgery at 5 p.m., Diana looks quite worried.

"Can they make us have an injection?"

Confused at first, I'm not sure what she means. After a bit more tapping into the translator and a few words from Alya, who is walking with us and shaking her head nervously, I realise she means a Covid vaccination.

I sigh and reply, "No, they can't make you do anything, but why would you not want to be protected?" I realise this is not the time to have a debate about the rights and wrongs of vaccinations and again I'm aware of holding judgement on their beliefs.

Before we can go any further with this debate, we arrive at the surgery and I'm grateful when we are called in to see the G.P. almost immediately. I'm relieved that, after examining her, the G.P. does indeed confirm my thoughts and diagnosis and prescribes anti-inflammatory and pain relief medication and exercise, with no further treatment required.

As we stand at the pharmacy counter, I say, "That's good news; the tablets should make you feel better very soon."

I am shocked as Diana rather loudly says, "He is wrong – I need to see a specialist!"

I am so angry and feel embarrassed, I can barely speak to her on the walk home.

REFLECTION:

Now I have calmed down a little, I realise it must be very scary to be in a different country without the health care you are used to or trust in. My understanding of their culture and how different it is, is reinforced with the arrival of today's Amazon parcel – a litre plastic container of diluted hydrogen peroxide? I thought that was an old-fashioned way of bleaching hair until Diana tells me it is good to inhale for sinus problems. I'm slightly unnerved by this, although I am learning to give up my urge to argue and 'let it go.'

CHAPTER 32
THE SCHOOL UNIFORM

THURSDAY, 11TH AUGUST

I am getting used to Alya remaining in her room until around 4 p.m., when almost to the minute, she rushes into the kitchen with a stack of plates and cups to wash up just in time before Diana comes home from work. Some days I almost forget I have guests as I start my day's work – although this is not one of them, as in my lunch break I need to ensure that Alya is up and ready to meet with Julie, who hopefully will bring some positive news about the school place, along with some of the uniform she has ordered for Alya to try on.

When I knock on the door at 1 p.m., I'm pleased to see she is up, dressed and ready to meet with Julie.

"I am bored and want to go to school" she tells me via the translator as we wait.

When Julie arrives, she hands Alya a new blazer with the familiar blue piping of my granddaughter's school and a pair of black trousers for her to try on. She also brings lots of information Diana and Alya will need and a school website address where Alya can order school meals and messages to and from parents can be exchanged when she starts school after the summer break.

I decide to leave all the information for Diana and Alya to work out between them and try not to interfere too much as it will be a good way for Alya to improve her English – it is already becoming quite good.

Alya pulls and tugs as she struggles to make the blazer buttons meet and it is clear it is way too small. Her face reddens and she is evidently embarrassed.

"I am too fat," she says with a weak smile.

I suddenly feel very warm towards her as if she was my own daughter and try to make a joke about it being Rosso's fault for chewing the tape measure.

Julie apologises – although she makes matters worse when she says she thought a size 12 would be big enough so she ignored the measurements Diana had correctly sent to her! As I show her to the gate, I can't help myself as I tell her how thoughtless I think her words are. She promises to come back with the correct size but I don't think she realises how insensitive she has been.

I return to Alya, who is still upset, and spend some time chatting with her, asking her how she is feeling about going to school and if there are there any books she likes to read. She says she is scared that she will not be clever enough at the school and tells me her favourite book, one she has read many times.

"Mine too," I say, and I go to my bookcase and among the many and diverse titles I've collected over the years, fish out a tattered, well-read copy of *Alice In Wonderland* – I've kept it since my daughters were small.

Handing it to her, I say, "You can borrow it if you like?"

Later I see Alya is talking to my neighbour's guest's

son, Josyp, over the fence. I try to ignore the fact that she is holding Luna in her arms (having not received the results of the blood test yet). This is good, and even though I have no idea what they are saying, Alya is laughing and seems a lot happier.

As soon as Diana arrives home, Alya takes her mother's bike and sets off down the road with Tony my neighbour and Josyp. It's good to see her getting some exercise and fresh air.

REFLECTION:

How much Alya lacks confidence. I know lending her the book won't encourage her to come out of her room, but hopefully it will give her some comfort when she immerses herself in the strange world of Alice. Now we have a shared connection! I'm so pleased she will be going to my granddaughter's school too.

CHAPTER 33
THE ARGUMENT

FRIDAY, 12TH AUGUST

I am in the shower. It is 7.30 a.m. and I can hear distant shouting. It's hard to make out at first and I think it is someone shouting at their dog in the street until it gradually dawns on me it is coming from my back yard.

Drying myself quickly, I pull on my fluffy white towelling bath robe, step into my slippers and wrap a small pink hand towel around my head. I probably look quite a sight, although my garden is not overlooked so I don't mind going outside dressed like this on what – even at this time of the morning – is already quite a warm summer's day.

I now see where the commotion is coming from. Diana is on her knees, frantically trying to pump up her bike tyre, looking up every now and again to emit a string of words in Ukrainian at Alya, who is standing in her nightie, rubbing her eyes as she tries to adjust to the light this early in the morning (for her) and looking very sorry for herself.

"Diana, what's happened?"

Diana: "This child!!"

Trying to lighten the atmosphere, I wink at Alya, saying, "She looks more like a little mole."

Alya smiles ruefully. Diana doesn't as she carries on feverishly pumping at the tyre.

Eventually, Diana gives up and collapses in the garden chair, defeated. "I cannot go to work today!

Alya tiptoes back to their room as if she's trying not to be noticed.

It's too early for wine, although I could do with one as I sit in the other chair beside her. It turns out Alya, when she borrowed the bike, has adjusted the saddle (she is much shorter than Diana), lost the spanner, and on top of all that, the tyre has gone down again. I offer to take her to the cycle shop as I have no clients today.

She declines with, "I probably won't go anywhere today," followed by a rather sheepish, "but thanks for the offer."

As she walks awkwardly to her room, vigorously rubbing her back, she turns to me and adds, "I need a car!"

I've learnt from previous experience to just 'leave it' when things get heated, so I get dressed, dry my hair and go shopping. I'm going out for the day on Sunday – a welcome break.

However – rightly or wrongly – when I get in the car, I feel obliged to call her manager to let him know she's not coming in to work. She's already messaged him and he is concerned whether there is anything he can do to help her. He agrees to ensure the table she works at is raised to accommodate her height and hopefully ease her back ache a little.

REFLECTION:

My first experience of Diana and Alya's conflict – normal of course in families – but this family has so much added tension given what's happening back at their home in Ukraine. It's reassuring to hear her employer is acting responsibly and aware of her health and safety. She is lucky to have found such a job and I feel for her because I know it's not what she is used to. I'm imagining she feels a little embarrassed at my witnessing their upset.

CHAPTER 34
THE FLOWERS

SATURDAY, 13TH AUGUST

I decide we all need a bit of a break today to recuperate and I suggest a visit to our local garden centre. Diana is in her element, as she loves plants and flowers as much as I do. As we walk around with Rosso in tow, she spots her favourite, a pot orchid, and buys it. She helps me choose some bedding plants for a wheelbarrow planter in my garden.

We enjoy a coffee and cake in the café before going home to plant up the wheelbarrow. Diana and Alya seem amused when I won't let Rosso off the lead. They don't seem to mind him jumping up and running around and tell me that at home in Ukraine, there are fewer dogs kept as house pets but there are many 'street dogs' roaming around who everyone feeds and looks after.

The plants are not ones I would have chosen on my own but I'm surprised at how good they look when she arranges them in the barrow – she clearly has a good eye for design. As she reaches for the hose to water her handiwork, this seems a good time to 'talk water.'

I speak into the translator. "It is not necessary to water the garden with tap water. We can always use the washing up water instead of throwing it away."

"WHY?"

"Water is expensive here and as usual in summer, we face a drought and a hosepipe ban."

And while I have her attention. "Do you think you could only use the washing machine when you have a full load?"

"In Ukraine, we don't pay for water."

I'm not expecting this response and resist the temptation to say any more than, "Well unfortunately, we do here and it is very expensive." I can see how surprised she is.

Later, I'm feeling a bit mean about my words and I manage to find a spare electric fan and take it to their room – it is very warm in there and they are both fast asleep.

I have a hunt around in the greenhouse – I'm sure I remember putting a packet of sunflower seeds bought earlier in the year there. I find them and make a note to give them to Diana as a peace offering to plant in the garden.

REFLECTION:

I'm fascinated to hear about how dogs are viewed in Ukraine. I guess this explains why they are so relaxed about the rabies rules and possibly why the disease is still worryingly common in Ukraine. Hopefully the sunflowers will be like a little bit of home.

CHAPTER 35
THE BURP PART II

SUNDAY, 14TH AUGUST

This evening, I return home from my day out feeling refreshed and notice that there is an Amazon parcel for Diana tucked under the hedge by the side gate. I take it in to her and we chat about our respective weekends. She is also looking much calmer, having rested for the weekend. I guess we have both enjoyed the break away from each other.

She opens the parcel – it's a puncture repair kit, a spanner and I assume other bike related gadgets, although I've no idea what they are for. Just as I am going back to the house to unpack, Diana calls me back, waving her mobile phone in the air.

"What is this?"

I don't feel like starting an all too familiar lengthy question and answer session but I suppose I'd better have a quick look – it might be important.

In my kitchen, we sit at the table and I try to make sense of the message on her phone. Finally, it gradually dawns on me – it seems at some point on her travels from Ukraine, Diana has already made an application for the Burp! I can hardly believe it – all that painstaking work we put in to complete the application and she has already done it. So where is the Burp now?

REFLECTION:

I admire Diana's stalwart independence and resourcefulness in ordering the repair kit. I feel a little guilty for not giving her credit for this. I sense Diana is concerned about being a burden and this sometimes leads to her not sharing information and trying to do everything herself so we are often duplicating tasks. It suddenly dawns on me why she didn't seem bothered about the journey to Sheffield. I think she already knew she would need to go there. I'm too tired to even feel annoyed – tomorrow promises another day of trying to untangle more complex paperwork.

There's more to this hosting than I ever imagined. My fears of having people 'in my space' is now the least of my worries. I think my brain will explode with all the testing paperwork!

CHAPTER 36
THE DETECTIVE WORK

MONDAY, 15TH AUGUST

I'm not looking forward to spending my precious moments in between my client sessions trying to locate the Burp! I discover it has been sent to a post office somewhere in the centre of Sheffield. I have to call around six post offices – they are all very busy and take ages to answer – only to find out after much 'Googling' that the post office I need is above a hardware shop and doesn't appear to have a phone number of its own.

On phoning the hardware shop, I discover that they have a private number for the post office which they eventually agree to give to me, along with the negative comment, "They probably won't answer; they are very busy." I'm beginning to wonder if there is anyone in Sheffield who isn't 'very busy' but I can't give up now.

I keep trying and after four failed attempts, they eventually pick up and I tell the story to the very kind sounding man on the other end – probably with rather more embellishments than are necessary to let him know how difficult all this is for me. I spell out Diana and Alya's surnames and names (their surnames are different as Diana is divorced), trying to do it using the phonetic alphabet, but giving up when I get to the first 'V'. Having tried 'volcano' and 'Volvo', I resort to just speaking louder and emphasising each letter as I spell, hoping this helps.

He puts me on hold, with the hold music being the best part of the whole experience as it's my very favourite Stevie Wonder song, so I sing along while he searches. Just as I'm picturing him going through endless dusty files in an attic room, he comes back and very matter-of-factly says, "Yes, they're here."

"Are you sure?" I ask rather sarcastically. Quickly moving on to, "Oh, that's brilliant. Let me give you my address so you can post them out to my guests."

I start to tell him my address and he interrupts me by saying, "Oh no, we can't post them. They'll have to come and collect them and bring ID."

REFLECTION:

AAAARGH!

CHAPTER 37

THE FUN

SUNDAY, 21ST AUGUST

Surprisingly, this afternoon the Amazon parcel that arrives is for me! It is a large cardboard box and for a minute I forget what I've ordered with all the recent distractions. I open it carefully and peek inside, delighted to see it is the print copies of my recently published book, *Reflections From A Narrowboat*. It's my first book – I've not actually held a copy in my hands as yet, and it is a wonderful feeling.

Diana and Alya come through the kitchen; they're off for a walk to the local shop. I excitedly show them the book and they are excited too.

"You wrote this?" Diana asks wide-eyed.

"Yes, it's my first book," I reply proudly. I look at Alya and ask, "Would you like to be the first person to have a signed copy?"

"For me?" She smiles, her eyebrows raised in surprise.

Diana offers to photograph me as I am signing the book and I dedicate it to Alya. She then takes lots more photos and sends them to her mother, who immediately calls via video. She is excited too and I think she is congratulating me in Ukrainian – although I can't be sure. We are all dancing around my kitchen and laughing.

I point to the cover of my book and say, "Narrowboat?" with an upward inflection at the end to turn the word into a question. Diana and Alya look puzzled so I speak into the translator to explain, then add, "I often hear you say a word that sounds like 'narrowboaty'. What does it mean in Ukrainian?"

It takes a while to get them to understand but in the end, I learn it means 'going to work'.

Alya points to a few other things, naming them in Ukrainian, and I reply with the English equivalent and practice repeating the Ukrainian words phonetically. They both are in fits of laughter at my efforts.

'Stilets' – chair.

'Polyta' – cooker.

'Kholodylnyk' – refrigerator.

'Tak' – yes.

I do the same in reverse and point to Luna, who I see through the window is sitting on the step outside their room, safe now having had the 'all clear' from her blood test. They both laugh again, and apparently with my accent, the way I say 'Luna' in Ukrainian means 'monthly cycle'.

When they come back from the shop, I ask if they could help me make a video of me opening my delivery of the books for my social media promotion (suggested by my editor). I set up the box on the table in the garden and close it again so I can pretend I am opening it for the first time. I pour us both a glass of wine as Diana finds a good position with the sun behind her and fiddles with my phone to prepare to start the video.

"Ready?" I ask with my hands poised above the box.

In broken English, she says, "Oh, what is in the box?"

"It is my new book," I reply.

It sounds so funny and stilted. We are both giggling so much that we have to do three more 'takes' before we can do it without laughing.

When we are satisfied with the result, we sit and chat for a bit longer. It is great to be able to share humour with my guests and Diana tells me that before they came to England they were told, "The English like to laugh at themselves."

Later, I take another electric fan into their room. It is still very hot, even this late in the evening. Diana pauses from her phone call, taking out her earpods to thank me.

"Everything OK?" I ask.

"I am so worried for my mom."

I feel sad for her, and remembering my verbal clumsiness at our very first video meeting, I reply, "I wish there was something I could say to reassure you."

She smiles forlornly, and showing that strength I have become used to seeing in her, says, "Don't worry, be happy."

REFLECTION:

I've learnt my first words in Ukrainian! I'm sure it's more difficult than English but I don't think Diana and Alya will agree. What a day of mixed emotions!

CHAPTER 38
THE BIRDS

MONDAY, 22ND AUGUST

Julie is coming back today to take Alya and Diana for a look around the school and hopefully bring the correct sized uniform. It's going to be a bit of a rush as Diana won't be home until five o'clock and the few teachers that will be at the school will be leaving shortly after that.

I think it will be good to have a quick look around in the school holidays before the possible pressure of her first day.

I am in between online clients when Julie arrives and I can hear Diana, who has just arrived home, from the back door shouting at Alya in their room – I presume she is telling her to hurry up. I also want her to hurry as I need to get back onto my next client call and Rosso won't settle when there's all this activity with visitors going on.

Diana and Julie walk towards Julie's car and get in. Diana is saying something angrily in Ukrainian, then very clearly in English, "OH THAT CHILD!!" She is plainly concerned not to keep Julie waiting and frustrated with

Alya, who still hasn't come out from their room, so I go to see what's going on.

Alya, still shoeless, is cupping a tiny baby bird in her hands, whispering tenderly to it. I feel despairing but she's evidently going nowhere until we can save the life of the bird.

"How about we put him in the garden, somewhere safe from the cats?" I ask hopefully.

"No, he can't fly. He has lost his mom," she replies tearfully.

I hold out my cupped hands and indicate that I will find somewhere safe, carefully taking the tiny creature from her, and signal that she should put her shoes on. I climb up onto a wobbly garden chair and manage to put the quivering bird almost in the centre of the low flat roof of the outside toilet where I hope my cats don't go.

Alya comes out and just as I am explaining that the bird's mother will surely see it there, with a bit of wobbly fluttering, the little bird soars off into the distance and disappears behind the houses. Alya gets into Julie's car. I breathe a sigh of relief.

It is now five minutes before my next client logs on and I realise I have been so busy, I haven't had time to check on my chickens today. I rush down the garden, take some handfuls of corn (their evening treat) from the bin in the shed, and throw it into their run. I love to watch them all come running up to get their food – a quick way of getting them back from the garden, where they've been free-ranging, to securely lock them up for the night, safe from foxes and other predators. Quickly bolting the gate of the run, I think there is one missing. A quick head count confirms my fears and I scan the garden.

I see poor Harriet under the hedge, head tucked under her wing in true chicken death pose. There is no time for sentiment as I find an empty plastic chicken feed bag and scoop up her body into it, then place it into a second bag, and into the bin in the yard. I go back to work with a heavy heart and a little sad I don't have time to give Harriet the burial she deserves.

I've felt a little unwell myself all day and very tired. Now I've managed to get through my day's work, I'm feeling a bit worse and wondering what is wrong. I've had no opportunity to call my G.P. for advice so I dial the number at about 6 p.m. and when they eventually answer (45 minutes later) they tell me that the next available appointment is in two weeks' time, and if it's an emergency to go to A&E. It doesn't feel like an emergency but as I wait, the pain in my side gets worse and I'm not so sure, so I decide to call 111 – the non-emergency NHS number. My daughter who lives nearby is away and I'm feeling quite alone as I wait on the phone for at least an hour for a response. It's such a relief to hear a voice which asks me for my medical history and current symptoms. The voice is very apologetic when she tells me there has been a cyber attack on the computer system and she has to take all the information by hand. She agrees that I need to see a doctor and gives me a number to call which is connected to my local hospital to arrange a visit to an out-of-hours G.P. I call the number but it is the general switchboard number and they know nothing about an out of hours G.P. contact.

9.30 p.m. and the pain is still there. I am getting scared. I call back 111 and they give me another phone number – this time the correct one – so I call them and they ask me to come in. It is about a five-mile drive. The G.P. examines me and prescribes some medication, then the receptionist directs me to the all-night Tesco which has a pharmacy counter.

It's 10.30 p.m. when I park up and try to go into the store through the automatic night-time entrance door but it doesn't seem to be working. There are a couple of cars in the car park and I can see through the window that staff are stacking shelves, but all my frantic banging on the thick glass and shouting doesn't manage to get their attention. I do a bit of a dance around the other side of the window – as much as my increasing pain in my side will allow – waving my arms around maniacally. After about five minutes, one of the shelf stackers saunters outside.

I'm quite out of breath from all the bobbing up and down and waving and I explain what I'm looking for as he leans casually against the window. In between strong draws on his e-cigarette, he tells me the door is always sticking and it works perfectly well from the inside. He doesn't know where I got the information from, concluding with, "The pharmacy here isn't open tonight."

I'm clearly intruding on his vape break, and without speaking further, he beckons me to follow him round to the other door, pointing to a card tucked into the corner. I can just make out from the faded handwriting the address of the late night pharmacy on call. Luckily, it is on my way home, as they close at 11 p.m. and it's now 10.45 p.m.

I eventually collect my prescription and drive home. Rosso is confused as his routine is disrupted – he hasn't had his walk this evening and wonders where I've been. I take him for a very quick walk around the block and eventually fall into bed, exhausted at 11.45 p.m. – way past both of our bedtimes.

REFLECTION:

I'm giving this hosting my all and not caring for myself enough.

I can't believe I've gone all day with this pain and not found time to contact the doctor. I wanted to tell Diana where I was going but she has enough to worry about.

CHAPTER 39
THE 111

TUESDAY, 23RD AUGUST

I feel like I need to take it a bit easy today after yesterday's late night adventure and I'm hoping my medication starts to work very soon. Today will be an easy day at work. Diana has thankfully gone to work too – I'm always a little on edge, worrying she might lose her job if she isn't able to go in regularly due to illness. She has already lost a day due to the puncture and one with her back pain and she has not been in the job long enough to warrant sick pay. However she is made of strong stuff.

I put a message request on the Facebook page to see if anyone might be travelling up to Sheffield and could give Diana and Alya a lift to collect their Burps, but there is no luck with my request.

However, just before lunch, a response comes in from a woman who has looked into this issue for her guests, and she tells me there is information on the government website which describes a way in which the Burps can be sent directly to you if you have provided relevant ID.

Sending off a brief email, I'm hopeful this will solve what feels like the last step of the mountain of paperwork and there will be nothing else to do in securing Diana and Alya's residency.

After seeing my first two clients of the day, I go back to the house to get some lunch. I'm just about to take a bite out of my sandwich when the doorbell goes at the side entrance. Thinking I've probably made an error with appointment times – a fairly regular occurrence for me – I go to answer the door prepared with an apology.

Diana is standing there, looking very pale, and I see behind her a car drive away down the street.

"I am unwell." she tells me in a trembly voice and pushes past me, walking towards their room where she falls back onto her bed with a huge sigh and "I need sleep."

Trying to establish what is wrong is difficult as she points to her chest and also says she has a pain in her arm. Now I'm really concerned, aware that these could be symptoms of a heart attack.

"I'll call the doctor," I say anxiously but she says "No" very loudly, followed by, "All I need is sleep. Alya will help me."

She is getting more distressed and Alya is looking worried. I am expecting my next client shortly – the first of three over the afternoon – so I decide to let her sleep and keep checking on her in between. The first two checks show her asleep and her colour and breathing seem OK. My final client cancels at short notice, and when I go in at 3 p.m., Diana is awake and sitting up in bed.

"How are you feeling?"

"I have a pain in my head and here." She points to her chest.

Unable to relax until I get some reassurance – although not feeling too confident after last night's experience – and despite Diana's protests, I insist on calling 111. When the woman on the other end answers, I launch into explaining what has happened.

"Are you with the patient?" she asks.

As I look at Diana, she falls back heavily into her pillows, still looking pale and exhausted. I realise she doesn't understand who I'm calling, so I speak into the translator, asking, "Is it OK to talk to the doctor about your pain?" Diana nods wearily. Returning to the phone assessor, I say, "Yes, she doesn't speak English so I have her consent to speak to you on her behalf."

"Unfortunately, I need to speak to the patient directly to carry out my assessment."

"Then you will have to find an interpreter," I say, probably more loudly than I intended.

She agrees and puts me on hold for what seems like ages, and then comes back with another woman and they work together to begin the assessment. First they ask me the question in English and then I hold the phone for Diana to answer the interpreter in Ukrainian.

The questions about Diana's medical history and current symptoms seem endless. It is boiling hot in the room, even with the fan going full pelt next to her bed, and I'm getting increasingly worried, looking at her face as she grimaces and sighs, that her pain seems to be getting worse.

After 45 minutes of repetitive questioning, in my anxiety, I finally snap when the assessor asks, "Are you feeling hot?"

"We are all feeling hot. It is over 30 degrees in here!" I spit impatiently down the phone. "This conversation is getting us nowhere. I'm going to call 999."

An ambulance arrives after about an hour with two women crew— from their lanyards, I note one is a paramedic and the other an emergency care technician. They work swiftly and calmly, going through the assessment and recording vital signs, with me assisting them to use the phone translator to communicate with Diana. We even manage a bit of a laugh and they are very kind and reassuring to Alya, chatting about Luna. Amazingly, one of them shows us a photo on her phone of her cat, which is the same rare breed as Luna, so this gets Alya interested and distracts her a little.

I am bracing myself for her reaction as I feel sure that they will want to take Diana to hospital for further tests. They discuss every result of their tests carefully in making their decision.

Eventually, the more senior one of the two women sits down on the bottom of Diana's bed and breaks the news I have been dreading. Diana responds much as I expect, and still attached to the monitor, she sits bolt upright in bed.

"I am feeling better now!"

The crew laugh as they see on the monitor that her heart rate, which has been very slow (this is what some of the concerns have been about), rises rapidly.

Diana smiles hopefully. "There, you see. I am well again."

We all make sympathetic noises, although I am determined and stress she cannot stay here until she has had further tests and the risks of her condition worsening are ruled out. Feeling much more confident and supported with the ambulance crew here, and knowing that I'd have a bit of 'authority' to back me up in convincing Diana she needed to go to hospital, helped in my feeling much less the 'baddie'.

It's now 5.30 p.m. and she gives in with only a feeble protest of a fight and is escorted to the ambulance with

Alya alongside. I tell them I will stay here and can collect her when she has been seen at the hospital.

I breathe a sigh of relief that she is now in good hands, for the time being at least. Not having much of an appetite, I make myself a quick snack – a bowl of tomato soup with some crusty bread, my favourite when I am needing a bit of nurturing. I realise, aside from all of Diana's drama, I'm still not feeling great myself. I settle down in front of the TV with the bowl of soup on a tray on my knee, although not concentrating on the programme as I'm waiting for a message from Diana, knowing I'll be going out again to collect them at some point.

Text messages from The Hospital Car Park

Diana 19:36
We are very hungry, but we don't know when they will let us go...

Me 19:38
Would you like me to cook something for when you come home?

Diana 19:39
Oh yes!!!! We are still sitting in the car!

Me 19:39
In the ambulance?

Diana 19:39
Yes.

Diana 19:40
I feel better and want to run away home.

Me 19:40
Call me when you are ready. I messaged
Alya but I don't think she got? X

Diana 21:28
We are still waiting, although the doctor has
already arrived.

Me 21:28
Ah, are you in the hospital?

Diana 21:29
We are sitting in an ambulance.

Me 21:30
So does the doctor come out to you?

Diana 21:41
A little more and I'll just turn around and
leave... I can't take it anymore... this is
some kind of bullying. We have been
waiting for five hours.

Me 21:41
It is normal. Our health service is in crisis.

Diana 21:45
It's already ten o'clock!!!!!! They don't even
know when they will accept me!!!!!

Me 21:45
I know!

Diana 21:53
Ali's phone went dead. and my phone is
almost out of battery.

Me 21:54
Didn't Alya take her charger?

Diana 21:55
Perhaps you should leave for us, because there may be no connection. And I said that I will wait another 20 minutes and that's it. I am very tired!!! This is not help or treatment...

Me 21:56
Turn off your phone and just use it to tell me when you have been seen.

Diana 21:56
We tried to connect the charger but it didn't work.

Me 21:56
You will be seen and need your blood tests.

Diana 21:58
If nothing changes within 20 minutes, we go home.

Diana 22:43
There are so many people here that I won't get here until morning. We are going to go. I won't wait any longer.

Me 22:43
Are you in the hospital?

Diana 22:44
Yes. We are where we were.

Me 22:44
In the emergency department now not the ambulance?

Diana 22:46
General Hospital Accident And Emergency Department.

Me 22:46
Can you ask at the desk if they have any idea how long?

Diana 22:47
I already asked. No one knows anything for the sixth hour. I've had enough.

Me 22:48
OK. Will you wait outside the main entrance?

Diana 22:50
We are from the ambulance side. I don't know where the main entrance is.

Me 22:50
That is it. Please tell them you have decided to go.

Diana 22:53
I already said.

Reluctantly, I feel there is no choice but to collect them. I take the phone charger and Diana's purse from their room and start the drive to the hospital, which shouldn't take more than 20 minutes at this time of night.

Ping! I hazardously glance down at my phone. It's blinking rapidly in its car charger.

Diana 22:56
It's kind of crazy. They just came and said that they would accept me in 5 minutes.

I decide to continue in any case as at least I can find out more information about what is happening. As I pull into the hospital car park, I am shocked to see all the ambulances lined up by the entrance. I park up and start to walk towards the main doors. As I get closer, I see that all the ambulances have their rear doors open with their waiting patients inside – some on stretchers, some seated with their heads in their hands.

I've heard about it on the news but nothing can prepare me for the sight that awaits me when I walk into the A and E department. Pale, sick looking people in wheelchairs with a friend or relative crouched on the floor beside them as there are no free chairs. People alone on trolleys with staff attending to them in full view of everyone. All the private cubicles are occupied with curtains drawn around them. More bodies sit on the floor around the edge of the department, propped up against the wall. Some wearing face masks but most not. I'm trying not to think about the risk of Covid infection spreading in this place with hardly a foot of space between the waiting patients.

I can't see Diana in the crowd, then she messages me.

Diana 23:10
We have just been taken for tests.

Alya appears from somewhere, looking completely lost. I give her a hug and tell her to try not to worry. I wait in the queue at the reception desk, and when it's my turn, I ask if they have any idea how long Diana might be. The harassed looking receptionist tells me it could be hours yet.

Alya and I walk around outside for a while as I can't bear to stay in here any longer; it is too upsetting and it must be scary for Alya. I chat with some of the paramedics who are so frustrated having to wait – not being able to attend to any more emergency calls. I message Diana again.

> **Me 23:41**
> Are you nearly ready?

> **Diana 23:49**
> I will now have a cardiogram ... 10-15 minutes.

> **Diana 23:50**
> They are not released without a cardiogram.

> **Me 23:52**
> I am taking Alya home. Can you get a taxi? Message me when you are on your way. I will leave your purse and phone charger on the reception desk.

I take Alya home and pop a pizza in the oven – the quickest thing I can think of to cook at this time of night.

At 2 a.m. Rosso barks loudly. I'm not really sleeping. It makes me jump out of bed and I go to the side gate where Diana is waiting, having come back in a taxi. Alya is there too in her nightie, looking very pleased to see her mum is safe. They hug and walk to their room, exhausted.

REFLECTION:

What a horrible experience for them both! I am shocked at seeing for myself what an absolute mess our health service is in.

CHAPTER 40
THE REST DAY

WEDNESDAY, 24TH AUGUST

I feel like staying in bed today for fear of something else happening but I can't as I need to see clients. I'm feeling a little better physically as the medication is starting to help.

I don't see Diana and Alya all day, apart from when I go in to check how Diana is and to see if they need anything. She is also feeling better and is catching up on sleep mostly, I imagine, after the traumatic events of last night.

Later in the evening, she comes out into the garden and we sit and chat a little. She is clearly upset still and can't believe – as I can't – how awful the experience was at the hospital. She is not really able to understand or explain the outcome of the tests, but from what I can make out, she will get a letter with a consultant appointment to follow up and they are not overly concerned that there is anything serious wrong, thank goodness.

REFLECTION:

I can fully understand her reluctance and loss of trust in our NHS after her experience. I'm feeling quite concerned myself at the reality that being taken ill with no-one available to help. Comforted myself by watching 'Doc Martin' and reminiscing about how things used to be when you could call the doctors and they would visit you at home the same day. Feeling old and vulnerable. Can only imagine how Diana and Alya might be feeling.

CHAPTER 41
THE LOOSE ENDS

THURSDAY, 25TH AUGUST

Diana is back at work today. I take her in the car this morning as her bike is there because she got a lift home from a colleague on Tuesday.

My working day is as busy as ever. Alya comes into the kitchen with her arms full with a stack of washing up. Carefully arranging it on the draining board, she tells me she is feeling really bored now and can't wait to go to school, although she is nervous because she fears she may not be able to keep up with the work if her English doesn't improve. I try to reassure her, although secretly I'm wondering if the school will be fully supportive and understanding of her needs. It's a relief that the second uniform Julie brought now fits perfectly and we chat about possible shops nearby where she can go with her mum at the weekend to get all the other essentials she will need like shoes, a bag, pens, etc.

Still no sign of the outcome of the Child Benefit claim though, and I'm wondering how Diana will find the money to buy all these things for Alya – particularly the shoes, which I recall from when my own children were small, were always a real struggle to afford. I make a note to myself to remind me to offer to go with them at the weekend on the 'school shop'. However I think I may be underestimating Diana's financial management skills. I imagine she goes without a lot herself in order to give Alya what she wants and needs and also manages to send money home – something very important to her.

A few other issues are resolved: Alya's passport is returned in the post, meaning we can finally send a screenshot off by email to enable the Burp to be posted here. Alya also receives her school bus pass, meaning she can travel to and from school free of charge.

REFLECTION:

On the few shopping trips I've accompanied Diana and Alya since the day they arrived here, I've tried to guide them to the shops I think are the best value. I'm never sure if I am intervening too much in the way they spend their money. However, from what I've seen of Diana, I'm starting to understand how financially astute she is.

Overall, I sense things are settling a little and I hope we won't have to face any more dramas.

CHAPTER 42
THE LEAK

MONDAY, 29TH AUGUST

Bank holiday Monday and neither of us are working today. We potter around doing nothing very much, with occasional breaks to talk about nothing very much. I take Rosso for a walk, asking Alya if she wants to come but she declines. I think she's found a new computer game to play, much to Diana's concern as she has been given a couple of books to read from the school to prepare her before she starts next week.

After enjoying a peaceful walk across the field and through the woods, I return and the calm I left behind me is shattered.

"COME SEE QUICKLY – THERE IS FLOOD!"

I take a deep breath, hold it for six seconds and exhale loudly (I learned to do this at a meditation class a few years ago) as Diana takes me by the hand. Rosso, still on his lead, has no choice but to follow behind us. We all squeeze into the small shed outside where my guests' toilet is. Water is pouring from the cistern into the toilet and all our attempts to stop it by dislodging the stuck flush button are useless.

"I DON'T KNOW WHAT IS WRONG. I DO NOTHING!" Diana is understandably very upset now and there is not a lot of room in here as she gesticulates and then tries to pull the front from the boxed-in cistern. "We call someone?" she asks hopefully.

I'm not liking the idea of trying to explain via the translator that trying to get a plumber at any time is pretty hopeless, let alone on a Bank Holiday Monday. I settle for, "Please leave it alone and I'll see what I can do."

If I can't find a plumber, this means I'll need to leave the back door of the house open all night in case my guests need the toilet – not a prospect I feel comfortable with. If this was a standard toilet, I might be in with a chance of fixing it myself, but I've no idea what is wrong as this is a special type with the cistern and sink attached to save water and all neatly boxed in to save space. Clearly, we're not saving water now!

When I get into the relative calm of my kitchen, I vaguely remember that there is a retired plumber who lives nearby so I go round to see him in the hope he is home and can help. Fortunately, he is, and although he looks puzzled as I fail miserably to explain what I think is going wrong with the toilet, he kindly offers to come over and "have a look" – although it doesn't bode well as he admits that he has never come across such a "new-fangled toilet like this before."

An hour and a half later, we are still standing in the small space. Paul (the plumber) has scratched his head several times, Diana has gone back to their room (no doubt for a lie down after all the stress) and I learn more about Paul's family and the intricate detail about past toilets he has repaired than I really want to. Eventually, Paul manages to get to the well-hidden stop tap to turn it off and he leaves with the suggestion, "You'd best get a proper toilet," and under his breath, "I've buggered my back again now."

REFLECTION:

So much for the restful day – now I've got to find a plumber tomorrow!

CHAPTER 43
THE SCHOOL

MONDAY, 5TH SEPTEMBER

Alya, in her uniform, turns to pose for a photo which I proudly take on my phone as Diana goes with her this first morning so will be late cycling to work – even though I suggest she doesn't as there will be other children on the bus who will know each other from the previous term and I feel Alya may stand out if she turns up with her mum. However, Diana insists and Alya doesn't seem to mind. She tells me she has hardly slept as she is so nervous.

I'm quite looking forward to a day to myself but I think Rosso will miss her. He looks forward to her coming into the house and I often catch her brushing him and am surprised he lets her do it. She laughs when she has finished and he is all fluffed up. He is a very wilful puppy and she spoils him but I don't really mind – her love for animals is clear. This was obvious just yesterday when I was away. She messaged me and was very worried as she had noticed one of my cats – Lily – had developed an abscess that was giving her much pain. I rushed home to take her to the vets. Alya helped me to give her the tablets the vet had prescribed with no effort at all – very unusual for Lily not to protest and not an easy job on your own.

At 4 p.m. Alya returns home very excited, just as I get a call from the school's drama teacher (my name is down as a contact as Diana would not be able to take a phone call), asking if Alya would like to join the class on a school trip to the theatre in Leeds to see the play *Blood Brothers*.

REFLECTION:

Maybe I missed Alya being around more than I thought I would. I do hope she gets the grades she needs to be able to train to be a vet. I'm delighted to hear she is being welcomed and included in her new school.

CHAPTER 44
THE POWER CUT

THURSDAY, 8TH SEPTEMBER

The week is relatively uneventful so far – just the way I like it. Mostly, Diana and Alya are so tired after work and school that I don't see as much of them in the garden in the evenings as they tend to stay in their room.

This is fine by me as mostly all the paperwork is completed now and we are just left with the wait for the outcomes of our extensive form filling applications for Child Benefit – and of course, the arrival of the Burp. This is still causing Diana much angst. Understandably, she is worried that it may not arrive before her six months here is up and I constantly try to reassure her that it will come when it comes, trying and failing mostly to play down the added delays that may occur due to the postal strikes we are experiencing. This does not stop her telling me almost every day what I already know: "There are no mail for me?"

There is a chill in the air now autumn is almost upon us, and already my mind is turning to the massive heating bills I am expecting from the extra electricity being used by my guests. Just as I'm pondering on this and watching TV, the power goes off in the house. Almost immediately, Diana comes in to see what's going on. I take a look into the fuse box and see the switches for the sockets have automatically tripped. All I can think is something must be overloading.

We walk around to see if we can find what might have caused it, unplugging and re-plugging various items, but no luck. When we go into Diana and Alya's room, I notice the extension cable I provided is jam-packed full with their laptops, lamps and the fan, and runs to another extension cable and then to the main socket. In addition, it is still wrapped around the reel. Even with my limited electrical knowledge, I can see this is unsafe, so I tell Diana we need to unravel it. There are sufficient sockets in the room to accommodate all they need. Diana is not happy but she agrees that it needs to be safe and I agree to call an electrician in the morning. I flip the switch and power is restored.

REFLECTION:

It has just occurred to me that Diana may not realise that there is a different process involved between the still almost daily delivery of their Amazon parcels and the Royal Mail post delivery – hence the delay in the Burp delivery.

I appreciate Diana doesn't like my intrusion in telling her the room is not safe but I have to stand my ground and consider the safety of my property.

CHAPTER 45
THE MOUSE

FRIDAY, 9TH SEPTEMBER

The electrician duly arrives and the long process begins to identify the cause of the power cut. He calmly and systematically asks me to unplug every device and plug them back in one at a time to see what might trip the switches. Nothing seems to be the cause. Finally, he asks me to switch off the electric cooker, ignoring my protests that "We weren't using the cooker at the time." I climb precariously onto a kitchen chair and reach across the top of the kitchen wall cupboard to the far corner and flick the switch off and then on again.

"That's it!" he says smugly. "Something's gone wrong with the wiring in your cooker. Turn it off again and let's see what's going on in the box."

I step carefully down from the chair, we pull out the cooker and he uses a screwdriver to remove the front cover from the six-inch-long white plastic box that houses the wiring to the appliance.

"Well that's a first!" he says, stepping back and scratching his head. "Come and have a look at this."

I can't believe what I see. The body of a mouse is stretched out in the box, clearly his feast on my cooker wires dramatically interrupted by his untimely death by electrocution.

Looking at the electrician's face, I step in and offer, "Do you want me to remove it?"

"I'd rather *you* did," he says gratefully.

I pull on a pair of rubber gloves while he uses his phone to take a photo of the unusual incident – no doubt to share at the next electricians' convention. Half closing my eyes and turning away, I take a deep breath. With one hand, I quickly remove the poor rodent, holding it high in the air at arm's length while opening the lid of the bin with the other hand and dropping it to its final resting place. Gabriel and Lily look longingly from their cat beds as all hope of a potential snack disappear for ever.

While he replaces the chewed wiring, I realise uncomfortably that I owe Diana an apology.

REFLECTION:

Lovely to end the day with a laugh. I feel a bit closer to her as she graciously accepts my apology and I appreciate her sense of humour as, tapping into the translator, she says with a triumphant smile: "So I am the mouse?"

CHAPTER 46
THE COOKERY LESSON

THURSDAY, 15TH SEPTEMBER

> **Diana 18:38**
> Sometimes you don't have 20 pounds in cash?

> **Me 18:40**
> ? What's wrong?

> **Diana 18:41**
> 😄 Oh thank you, no need anymore. The problem is solved. Trying to get into fish and chips

I introduced Diana and Alya to fish and chips from our local shop in their first week here and although they loved them, they looked in horror at the big steaming pot of mushy peas in the corner of the shop and instead asked if they could have salad with their meal – this seemed very odd to me but with hindsight it sounds rather a nice change. I assume that's where they are sending the message from.

A little later, they come back disappointed with a pizza from the corner shop instead as it turns out the chip shop is closed. This is unusual for a Thursday so I take a quick walk down the road to have a look what's happened. There is a note on the door informing customers that the shop is closed due to staff illness. Of course, they couldn't read the notice.

Just when I am about to go to bed, Alya comes into the kitchen and asks if I have any sugar. I don't normally use it much but manage to find some and pour it into a little bowl. As she watches me do this, she is tapping into her phone 'some cornflour and eggs?' I'm beginning to wonder what is going on so I tap in 'Is this for school?'

She beams and says, "Yes, tomorrow we will make a cake."

"What sort of cake?" Hoping it is not one requiring many more ingredients. "Can you ask Mum what she has?" I say without thinking. Diana is probably less likely than me to have ingredients for a cake – and an English recipe at that.

"Oh no, she will kill me. It is late!" Alya replies.

Thinking, 'Yes, it is late and I'm tired,' but I don't want to cause any upset between them at this time of night – especially as Alya has a dentist appointment tomorrow after school and she is worried enough about that – I ask if she has a list. She is making an apple cake so needs apples (which I have plenty of in my garden), eggs (from my chickens) and butter and a container. The flour she can pick up from the corner shop on the way to the bus stop in the morning as I don't have any in the cupboard.

141

REFLECTION:

I am getting used to receiving random messages which don't always make sense at the time and find them quite amusing. I am reminded almost daily how difficult it must be for my guests to make sense of our English ways and traditions and what difficulties the language barrier can cause. I feel for Alya too – wanting to support her to 'fit in' at school as much as possible. I know how tough it is to feel different.

CHAPTER 47
THE DENTIST

FRIDAY, 16TH SEPTEMBER

I wait for Diana to come home from work and then take her to collect Alya from school and we set off to the dentist for their check ups. I want to be there to both help with the translation and the completion of the health check and consent to treatment forms. I'm also ready to deal with any further discriminatory comments from the receptionist, should they occur.

When completing Diana's form, I ask the question, "Do you drink alcohol?"

She laughs and shouts with false indignance, "No!"

"What about you, Alya?" I ask to lighten her mood a little more and take her mind off her visit.

We all laugh and settle with writing on Diana's form, 'Rarely'.

The rest of the visit is uneventful and the dentist is very patient and kind – although Alya is really nervous and every time he approaches her, she shouts out in a wobbly voice, "Ohhh," causing him to withdraw again. However, he manages somehow to examine her teeth and prescribe some special toothpaste along with the unwelcome news (with me translating every step of the way to reassure her) that she requires two small fillings at another future appointment. This gets the biggest 'ohhhhh' of all, but by this time he is already helping her up from the imposing dentist chair and ushering her out of the door. I imagine he is now behind and slightly harassed from exceeding the usual fifteen-minute slot available for check-ups.

REFLECTION:

Another hurdle overcome! It can be scary enough for anyone visiting the dentist – must be worse still when not speaking the same language.

CHAPTER 48
THE INDEPENDENCE

SATURDAY, 17TH SEPTEMBER

Diana and Alya are back from shopping this afternoon and they are very excited to show me their purchases. They have found a Polish shop which sells many things they couldn't originally find here in England, including some delicious looking Ukrainian chocolates, pickles, and most importantly of all, coffee!

We discuss the fact that Diana feels awkward using my kitchen and there is little space left in the fridge. I suggest buying a small fridge for their room and we go to look at some. I'm happy to lend the money until Diana gets paid next.

She also tells me she has booked a local driving instructor to give her a couple of refresher lessons and has paid to enrol on an online English course. When she shows me a sample of the course, it doesn't seem very good – the teacher uses lots of slang words and it is very Americanised. I try to explain my concerns but Diana says, "It is good."

I'm pleased for her - to see she her enthusiasm for learning.

REFLECTION:

I am surprised and impressed in how much they have achieved in their short time here. These seem like huge steps forward for them in helping to feel more at home. I guess I'll have to let them make their own mistakes but I find it hard to let go when I think they might be being cheated. Although they've only been with me for two months, it is clear that neither of us imagine completing the full six-month commitment we originally signed up for so maybe this might be a good time to start discussing the idea of finding a more permanent home, especially with the colder months coming. Their room can be so hot in the summer and cold in the winter. I can't believe it didn't occur to me before, but now I'm wondering with all the Ukrainians and other asylum seekers and refugees, will there be enough suitable accommodation available in this area? And there is Luna — not many landlords will take pets. We'd better start looking!

CHAPTER 49
THE DILEMMA

MONDAY, 19TH SEPTEMBER

Today, I contact the council to see what might be the best way forward to get accommodation arranged for Diana and Alya. My fears are confirmed. There is little available and appropriate social housing accommodation would be restricted to a one-bedroom apartment, and possibly not a ground floor one as older people and people with disabilities usually get priority with those. Apartments on the first floor do not usually allow pets. Even if we could find one that did, they are as rare as hen's teeth apparently, and Diana and Alya would not be a priority as it is understood (in the small print) that as part of the government scheme, they would be expected to stay with me for a minimum of six months.

I also look into the option of private landlords – which is even more unlikely. Apparently, there will need to be a guarantor to pay a deposit and the first (at least) three months' rent in advance as Diana hasn't built up a credit history. In addition, there are even fewer private landlords who accept pets.

I hear from the council that Diana can't even join the social housing list unless she is classed as homeless. I am told there is some sort of 'bidding' system where we can look at available properties on a website and then we can show our interest, but obviously, the successful applicants will be chosen based on need and if they meet the criteria. It is beginning to dawn on me that although we have managed here for these last few weeks, I am going to have to set a time limit for my hosting otherwise Diana and Alya will always be at the bottom of the housing list.

REFLECTION:

This feels like a difficult choice and I know I have to discuss things with Diana as soon as possible.

CHAPTER 50
THE SEARCH

TUESDAY, 20TH SEPTEMBER

My day is taken up researching the housing options. I have asked that Diana and Alya meet with me this evening – we adults are going to need a big glass of wine for this one!

Later, I try to explain via the translator that I'm not 'throwing them out', but in effect, I have to 'throw them out' in order to have any chance of finding their own accommodation. I'm not sure I'm doing a very good job of explaining but Diana responds first in a jokey way with a smile.

"You don't want us here?" Soon followed with her enthusiasm and some warming to the possibility of having more independence.

We look at the website and Diana is delighted to see a couple of properties in the nearby area that she would like. When we read the details, they are both one-bedroomed and neither take pets.

"WHY?" She exclaims, unable to understand.

I feel helpless to know how to explain about the social housing crisis in this country. Helping Diana sign up for daily alerts from the social housing website, I stress the importance of responding straight away by telling me as soon as she sees something that looks possible.

We then look into signing up for the Credit Union.[1] Diana is reluctant and it is difficult to explain that she could get a loan through them at a very low interest rate which would pay for a deposit and a bond, thus removing the need for a guarantor. It takes hours to understand, explain and complete all the forms, then Diana says she could get a loan from somewhere else.

REFLECTION:

This is the hardest thing I have experienced so far. It is difficult to show feelings via a translator and to be clear that I am thinking of their best interests. I feel sure the chances of getting social housing are slim so my message is delivered reluctantly. I'm worried Diana might take a loan out, be conned and lose money – although she is very determined to be independent, not wanting, I imagine, to be seen as a burden to me. I am so tempted to lend her the money for a private rental but I can't afford to. I can't see how this is going to be resolved.

. . .

1 *Credit unions are not-for-profit enterprises that enjoy tax-exempt status and are created, owned, and operated by their participants. They provide traditional banking services to their members, such as loans.*

CHAPTER 51
THE HOPE

SATURDAY, 1ST OCTOBER

Diana comes into the kitchen, excitedly waving her mobile phone around.

"There are two. This is my house!" she exclaims.

Taking her phone to look at what she is so excited about, I see a picture of a ground floor apartment just around the corner from my house! As I offer to help her submit her application, she tells me she has already done so.

REFLECTION:

I'm beginning to feel like I've failed by giving up my hosting before the expected six months is up.

However, on the other hand, I'm realising yet again that Diana is more capable than I first thought and my part is done in assisting them to get to the UK safely and in helping them to make a start with the work and school arrangements. It can't be easy for her either sharing a home with a relative stranger so I can understand her excitement at her forthcoming independence and I'm hoping she won't be disappointed, but having a horrible feeling she will.

CHAPTER 52
THE SURPRISE

MONDAY, 3RD OCTOBER

"We must go tonight!!" Diana exclaims, bursting through the side gate on her return from work.

Coming out of the back door, I almost collide with her in the narrow passageway at the side of my house, which is clearly not built to accommodate two adults and a bike.

When she calms down, I manage to interpret that the apartment let is now between herself and one more applicant. Carol, the council worker, has messaged to say it is important that Diana visits the property to confirm her interest in progressing the application and we need to meet her there at 5.15 p.m.

We quickly get changed and jump in the car, Alya carrying Luna – not a good idea in my opinion, but I settle on, "Well, I suppose it will be her home too."

Although the ground floor, centrally heated, double-glazed apartment is not in the best area of the village, and as we stand in the shared lobby, there is a distinctly unpleasant smell of stale cigarette smoke, when Carol opens the door to the apartment, I'm pleasantly surprised. The previous owner has left it in immaculate condition. There is a carpet in the lounge which Carol says they may leave, and everything is spotless.

Diana turns her nose up a little at the kitchen taps and asks if it is possible to replace them with a mixer tap. I try not to respond to what I think is a really trivial issue and concentrate on pointing out all the benefits in what I think is a really lovely apartment. A bath and shower (although Diana says, "We don't want a bath"), two bedrooms and the three spaces between the kitchen cupboards that will easily accommodate their fridge, a cooker and washing machine. A walk-in cupboard will effortlessly provide space for their bikes and be a useful hanging space for coats too.

Alya deposits Luna in the corner of one of the bedrooms where she stays for the entire visit. She talks to her as Diana and Carol chat in the kitchen. I go into the bedroom to see Alya and ask which bedroom she would like. She chooses the biggest but doesn't look too excited as she tells me, "Luna doesn't like it here." I launch into full estate agent sales pitch mode – concerned they might give up this (probably one chance) opportunity to find some decent accommodation because the cat 'doesn't like it.'

"Just remember how she was when you first came to stay with me; cats always take a while to settle down. She will be fine," I say, trying not to sound too desperate.

Luckily, Diana is already talking about what curtains she would like – so I think we have a 'sale' and I'm pleased I had the sense to bring what remains of my trusty tape measure. I distract Alya by asking her to help me measure up for a few fittings.

REFLECTION:

Can't help thinking they are going to be surprised when they experience the true cost of the utility bills here in the UK. I can hardly believe their good fortune in finding this gem of an apartment, and so quickly too. I'm pleased to see Diana's excitement, even taking into account Alya's (or Luna's) slight reluctance. I hope this is a real turning point for them – a new chapter.

CHAPTER 53
THE NIGHT BEFORE
THE MOVE

FRIDAY, 7TH OCTOBER

I suggest Diana and Alya sort out what they would like to take with them tomorrow. Diana shows me her phone, asking, "What is this?"

A text from another council worker – Sandra – informs her she will need to set up an account online in order to be able to access electric, hot water and the central heating. I log on to the utility company website and am asked for an account number, but there isn't an account number until I set up an account?

I quickly respond to Sandra's message and wait impatiently for a reply. The days are still bright but the evenings are quite chilly and I picture Diana and Alya feeling very cold and gloomy over the weekend without light, heat and hot water. I'm assuming she may have gone off duty early as it is Friday. She eventually gets back to me and suggests as it is now out of hours, I can use the chat facility on the utility company's website to ask a question or request a call back.

Logging in again, this time on Diana's phone, to my horror I see that I am number 425 in the queue! Waiting for a while and realising I have some work emails to attend to, I ask Diana to take her phone and come and let me know when the queue has gone down to around 6. An hour and a half later, she comes in and hands me her phone. I watch in anticipation for a few minutes as the queue goes down further.

6…5…4 then, "We are very busy with other customers and unable to answer at this time. Please try again later."

REFLECTION:

Unbelievable! Still, I can't help smiling to myself, thinking even at this late stage, we are still having admin problems – but not for much longer.

CHAPTER 54
THE MOVE

SATURDAY, 8TH OCTOBER

7 a.m. – very excited and preparing for a busy day ahead, I walk past the open door of the shed which houses my washing machine and see a huge overflowing pile of Diana's washing waiting in the basket. Before Diana can make a start on it – no messing with three items at a time today – I fill the machine to capacity and go along to their room to see how they are getting on.

It is another fine day with a gentle breeze. I suggest we start to move things outside ready for my friend to load the bigger items, including the fridge, into his van. This is the same friend – Richard - who helped me prepare for their arrival by moving my office to the bottom of the garden, laying some stepping stones to it, just three months ago.

We are moving stuff from their room in a methodical, organised way when the front doorbell rings and my calm demeanour is shattered by a burst of nervous energy that is my neighbour's guest Nadiya. She is waving her mobile phone around her head and almost jumping up and down as she asks, "I ask if you have any testicles for me?"

I'm completely flummoxed to begin with, and her gesticulations get more frantic in trying to make me understand. It doesn't help me as I can hear Diana shouting in Ukrainian at Alya from the back yard and I'm wondering what could have possibly gone wrong in the few seconds I've been away. After a poorly attempted chicken impression from Nadiya, I realise with some relief she is asking me if I have any eggs from my chickens. Not having the time for an English lesson, I quickly pop six eggs from my kitchen into a box for her, which seems to make her very happy, although she is still apologising and embarrassed as she backs out towards the gate.

Whatever the ruckus was in the yard it seems to have stopped and as I start to load up my car, I can't help being a little in awe of how much they have accumulated. I take Alya with me to help unload, although she spends most of the time with Luna on her lap in the car and laying on the floor playing with her when we arrive at the other end. I don't mind. I'm just pleased she's happy. Diana stays at my house to supervise the loading of the van.

In between trips to their new home, I take the washing out of the machine, peg it on the line and put another load in, feeling like I'm on autopilot as I carefully and systematically complete my mission to make this move go smoothly.

I arrive back at my house, having delivered the last load, and take in the final lot of washing from the line. It is all beautifully dry and I feel very satisfied as I fold it and place it in the basket, not to have wavered in my attempt to get things done in such an organised way. Finally, in my car ready for the final trip with Diana, she looks surprised when she sees the basket of washing – now neatly folded in the linen basket that I am giving her to keep.

"Thank you," she says as she smiles, "That was quick."

My friend refuses to accept any money for his time or petrol. I suddenly feel very emotional and give him a hug – again, gratitude overwhelms me at the kindness of people.

When we get to their apartment, we are pleased to see there is a considerable amount of credit on the electric meter and a message from Sandra tells us it will be OK to light the gas boiler and she will sort out the account on Monday. They will need beds, a cooker, a washing machine and already Diana wants a larger fridge – she says she had a huge one at home in Ukraine, not this "silly tiny one" – a good sign she wants to make this place 'home', for a while at least. But all that can wait for a few days.

Still no Burp – but they are in!

REFLECTION:

We have free tickets to see the pantomime in December. I won't tell them yet. Not sure what they'll make of it – with men dressed as women, women dressed as men and the typically British suggestive humour.

It seems strangely quiet as I set to clearing out my garden office and preparing to return to 'normal life' – although I know this experience has touched me greatly and things will never be the same. Diana's words come into my mind: "Don't worry – be happy". I do hope they are.

CHAPTER 55
THE HAPPY ENDING
(OR IS IT?)

So, three months to the day, Diana, Alya and Luna are safely in their new 'home'. However, this is far from a happy ending.

They never give up hope that one day soon they will be able to return to their real home in Ukraine and rebuild their lives there.

The sunflowers just didn't seem to flourish here in my garden this year – could be the lack of water but I see it as a sign that the UK is not – and probably never will – feel completely like 'home' for my Ukrainian guests and possibly all those forced to leave their natural home to seek safe refuge, no matter how hard we try to welcome them.

As I write, the war in Ukraine continues, along with many other wars across the world. Maybe a lesson can be learned from my hosting experience and from that of the thousands of other sponsors and supporters of refugees and asylum seekers – that it is possible to live in harmony and overcome difference if we can just be honest and kind.

CHAPTER 56
THE INTERVIEW

While writing this book, I visited Diana and Alya in their new home. Diana and I had a small glass of wine – a sweet Ukrainian one this time – and, with the help of our translator apps and with Diana and Alya's permission, I conducted an 'interview' to hear their reflections on their experience of being my guests and being in the UK generally.

Their answers are very revealing…

What was living in the Netherlands like before you came here?

Both: "Awful. We don't like big cities and it felt unsafe."

Diana: "There were brothels and marijuana and this is not good. We are religious."

Why did you want to come to the UK particularly?

Both: "Because we speak a little English and they spoke none in the countries we came through. It was horrible – we thought that England would be more accepting of us."

What did you look forward to most?

Diana: "I trusted God that all would be well."

What was your biggest worry when you were here?

Diana: "That we would be a burden to you." (this moved me greatly and explained a lot)

Alya: "I couldn't find friends."

Both: "We were upset with you for being unkind about the rabies."

Diana: "The hospital!!"

What did you find the strangest thing(s) about being here?

Diana: "We have to wait for everything!"

"The different rules."

"The fridge is sooo small."

"Stress of using water when we knew you didn't like it."

"Travelling on the left."

(FINAL) REFLECTION:

Feeling quite humble when hearing how concerned they were not to 'be a burden,' I can understand more, now the pressure is off, how some of my efforts to ensure our safety and well-being (particularly when trying to uphold the quarantine regulations) could have been misunderstood and be seen as cruel by Luna, Diana and Alya.

I've learned much about the Ukrainian culture – that in Ukraine, dogs are not only allowed to roam the streets, there are no laws that ban dogs being bred and trained to fight. This shocked me.

The hospital experience and Diana's frustration at having to 'wait for everything' rankled with me at the time as I feel the same about the lack of health services. I guess my concerns turned to direct impatience at my guests as I recognised my own helplessness to change things for them.

Given the language barriers and the cultural differences between us – both leading to my guests' vulnerability in a strange country – I find I am more understanding now about tolerating what to me are quite big differences between us, such as religious beliefs, how we view homosexuality and road safety rules.

'Our ways' are not 'their ways' and that is OK. I am learning to appreciate the assumptions and generalisations we make about cultures that are not our own do not help us to acknowledge that deep within 'our ways' and 'their ways' lies our individual truth about who we really are and that is more intricate than we could ever know.

Things will never be quite the same for me after my insight into this different culture. I have learned so much about myself in this process. I've developed more patience — most things are resolved eventually and others lose their importance after time.

"If there is righteousness in the heart, there will be beauty in the character. If there is beauty in the character, there will be harmony in the home. If there is harmony in the home, there will be order in the nations. When there is order in the nations, there will be peace in the world."

- Sathya Sai Baba.

ABOUT THE AUTHOR

From her home in a North Lincolnshire village, Alice White – the dyslexic author who can spell – manages a busy psychotherapy practice alongside caring for a menagerie of pets.

This is her second book in the *Reflections* series of memoirs.

Contact details:

**Look out for more stories and pictures on Facebook:
AliceWhiteWriterAuthor**

**or contact Alice at:
alicewhitewriter@outlook.com**

ACKNOWLEDGMENTS

Siân-Elin Flint-Freel for not hiding under your desk when I told you I was writing a second book and for supporting me to edit it with as much skill, knowledge and finesse as you did with my first.

Siân can be contacted on

sianelin.flintfreel@gmail.com

The talented and patient formatter Leanne can be contacted on

irishinkpublishing@gmail.com

Our local council staff – you know who you are – even with the additional work the 'Homes For Ukraine' Scheme imposed on you, you worked tirelessly to ensure my guests arrived and settled here and you continue to support them.

My family, friends and neighbours – bet you're wondering what I'm going to do next. 😉

Most importantly, to Diana and Alya for allowing me to write this part of your story.

Much love.

Printed in Great Britain
by Amazon